DISCARDED

HURON VALLEY PUBLIC LIBRARY
26336 EAST HURON RIVER DRIVE
FLAT ROCK, MICHIGAN 48134

641

Better Homes and Gardens®
After-School Cooking

HURON VALLEY PUBLIC LIBRARY
26336 EAST HURON RIVER DRIVE
FLAT ROCK, MICHIGAN 48134

Our seal assures you that every recipe in *After-School Cooking*
has been tested in the Better Homes and Gardens® Test Kitchen.
This means that each recipe is practical and reliable,
and meets our high standards of taste appeal.

BETTER HOMES AND GARDENS® BOOKS
Editor: Gerald M. Knox
Art Director: Ernest Shelton
Managing Editor: David A. Kirchner
Editorial Project Managers: James D. Blume, Marsha Jahns,
 Rosanne Weber Mattson, Mary Helen Schiltz

Department Head, Cook Books: Sharyl Heiken
Associate Department Heads: Sandra Granseth,
 Rosemary C. Hutchinson, Elizabeth Woolever
Senior Food Editors: Julia Malloy, Marcia Stanley,
 Joyce Trollope
Associate Food Editors: Linda Henry, Mary Major,
 Diana McMillen, Mary Jo Plutt, Maureen Powers,
 Martha Schiel, Linda Foley Woodrum
Test Kitchen: Director, Sharon Stilwell; Photo Studio Director,
 Janet Pittman; Home Economists: Lynn Blanchard, Jean Brekke,
 Kay Cargill, Marilyn Cornelius, Jennifer Darling,
 Maryellyn Krantz, Lynelle Munn, Dianna Nolin,
 Marge Steenson

Associate Art Directors: Linda Ford Vermie, Neoma Alt West,
 Randall Yontz
Assistant Art Directors: Lynda Haupert, Harijs Priekulis,
 Tom Wegner
Senior Graphic Designer: Darla Whipple-Frain
Graphic Designers: Mike Burns, Brian Wignall
Art Production: Director, John Berg; Associate, Joe Heuer;
 Office Manager, Emma Rediger

President, Book Group: Fred Stines
Vice President, General Manager: Jeramy Lanigan
Vice President, Retail Marketing: Jamie Martin
Vice President, Administrative Services: Rick Rundall

BETTER HOMES AND GARDENS® MAGAZINE
President, Magazine Group: James A. Autry
Vice President, Editorial Director: Doris Eby
Executive Director, Editorial Services: Duane L. Gregg
Food and Nutrition Editor: Nancy Byal

MEREDITH CORPORATE OFFICERS
Chairman of the Board: E.T. Meredith III
President: Robert A. Burnett
Executive Vice President: Jack D. Rehm

AFTER-SCHOOL COOKING
Editor: Maureen Powers
Editorial Project Manager: Marsha Jahns
Graphic Designer: Lynda Haupert
Electronic Text Processor: Paula Forest
Contributing Photographers: Wm. Hopkins, M. Jensen
 Photography, Inc.
Food Stylists: Janet Pittman, Maria Rolandelli
Contributing Illustrator: Thomas Rosborough

On the cover: Pie à la Mode Waffles
(see recipe, page 30)

Copyright © 1987 by Meredith Corporation, Des Moines, Iowa.
All Rights Reserved. Printed in the United States of America.
First Edition. Second Printing, 1988.
Library of Congress Catalog Card Number: 87-60053
ISBN: 0-696-01725-3 (Hardcover)
ISBN: 0-696-01727-X (Trade paperback)

Contents

4 School's Out!
Snazzy snack and supper tips for the after-class crew.

6 Quick Takes
Ready in less than 10 minutes, snacks that satisfy *now*.

20 Make-the-Grade Munchies
After-school goodies that rate an A+.

34 Twice-As-Nice Nibbles
Double-duty recipes you can munch now—and later as a different treat.

42 Make-Ahead Teasers, After-School Pleasers
Fix-ahead-and-store specials that are ready when you are.

50 Ready, Set, Start Supper
Suppers you put together, then let cook by themselves.

68 Mamma Mia, It's a Pizza!
A make-your-own pizza menu.

72 All for One and One for All
Sensational dinners everyone can enjoy, even those who work or play late.

90 Hero for a Day
A super sandwich supper that will make you the hero of the family.

94 Index

School's

Tackle after-school hungries two ways. First, join the snack team with one of our nourishing nibbles. They go great before homework, after practice, or anytime you need an extra energy boost. Or, try out for the dinnertime cooking crew and make a play for any of our delicious dinner dishes. Either way, your home team will cook up a big score!

First Things First!

Before you start cooking, take time to get organized so everything speeds along smoothly.

- Read over the recipe you've chosen to be sure you have all the ingredients.
- Set out all the ingredients and cooking utensils before you begin.
- If you're using the oven, turn it on to preheat before you start the recipe.
- If a recipe calls for a shredded, cut, or chopped ingredient, do this first.
- Always have hot pads handy when working with hot mixtures and hot utensils
- Try to clean up as you work. Rinse dishes and bowls and throw wrappers away.

Measuring liquids

A glass measuring cup is used to measure liquids such as milk, water, and juice. Place the cup on a level surface and bend down so your eyes are level with the correct marking. Fill the cup to the mark.

Measuring spoons
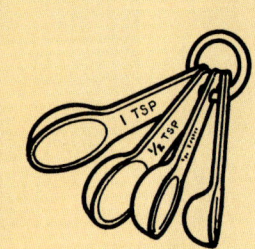
For small ingredient amounts, fill the correct measuring spoon to the top, keeping the ingredient level. If a recipe calls for ⅛ teaspoon and you don't have a ⅛-teaspoon measure, use *half* of a ¼-teaspoon measure.

Boiling vs. simmering
Boiling a liquid means that it's hot enough for bubbles to rise in a steady pattern and break on the surface. Simmering is cooking only until a few bubbles form and burst below the surface. When a recipe says to boil, then simmer, bring the mixture to a boil. Then, turn down the heat until the mixture simmers.

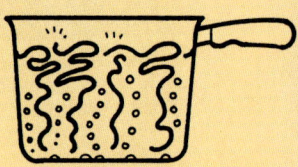
Boiling

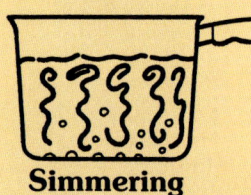
Simmering

Measuring dry ingredients

Be sure to use dry measures for ingredients such as flour, sugar, and rolled oats. Spoon the ingredient into the measure, then level it with a metal spatula. Never pack ingredients, except for brown sugar and shortening.

Shredding

When a recipe calls for a shredded ingredient, it means the food should be in long, narrow strips. Cheese, carrots, and zucchini are often shredded. To do this, rub the food against the shredder surface that has medium or large holes. To finely shred, rub the food against the smallest holes on your shredder.

Measuring margarine
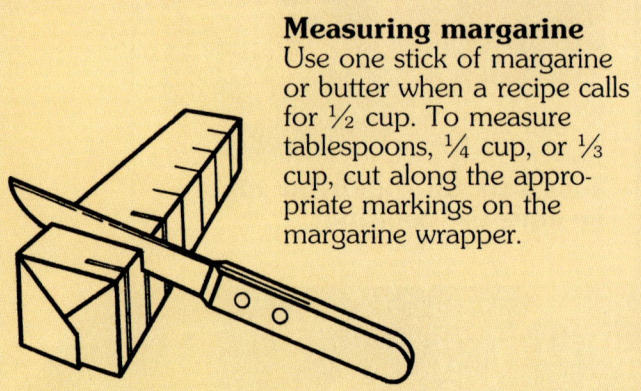
Use one stick of margarine or butter when a recipe calls for ½ cup. To measure tablespoons, ¼ cup, or ⅓ cup, cut along the appropriate markings on the margarine wrapper.

Quick Takes

Tic-Tac-Taco Mix

EQUIPMENT
dry measures
bowl
spoon
knife
small saucepan
measuring spoons

1¼ cups popped popcorn
½ cup bite-size shredded wheat biscuits
½ cup round toasted oat cereal

- In a bowl stir together popcorn, wheat biscuits, and oat cereal.

1 tablespoon margarine *or* butter
¼ teaspoon chili powder
Several dashes onion salt
Several dashes ground cumin

- In a small saucepan stir together margarine or butter, chili powder, onion salt, and cumin. Heat and stir till margarine is melted. Drizzle over cereal mixture; toss to mix. Makes 4 servings.

Make your own version of this mix by trying other unsweetened cereals instead of the oat cereal.

Fruit-and-Nut Nibble Mix

EQUIPMENT
dry measures
mixing bowl
spoon
airtight container

1½ cups granola
1 6-ounce package dried fruit bits
½ cup peanuts *or* chopped nuts
⅓ cup semisweet chocolate pieces (optional)

- In a mixing bowl stir together granola, fruit bits, and peanuts or nuts. Stir in chocolate pieces, if you like. Store in an airtight container. Makes about 3 cups.

Share a handful of this easy-to-fix, grab-a-crunch mix with a friend.

Peanut Butter Brigade

Firecrackers: Spread peanut butter on *graham crackers, mini-bagels, pita triangles,* or *tortillas.* Top with *candy pieces* or *coconut.*

Drum Rolls: Spread 2 tablespoons *peanut butter* over one 6- or 7-inch *flour tortilla.* Top with 1 tablespoon *apple butter, orange marmalade,* or any *jam* or *jelly.* If you like, sprinkle with 1 tablespoon chopped *apple, raisins,* or *sunflower nuts.* Roll up tortilla. (Or, fold it over and cut it into wedges.)

Fife and Drum Dip: Stir 2 tablespoons *peanut butter* and 1 tablespoon toasted *coconut* into one 8-ounce carton *vanilla yogurt.* Use as a dipper for *apple* or *pear slices* or *strawberries.* (Or, eat it plain.)

Cheese and Carrot Corps: Stir together ¼ cup whipped *cream cheese* and *peanut butter.* Add 2 tablespoons shredded *carrot.* Spread on toasted *raisin bread* or *bagels.*

Spirited Spread: Spread peanut butter on *banana, apple, peach,* or *cucumber slices* or *carrot* or *celery sticks.* (Or, if you like, skip the spreading and dip them!)

Dusty Popcorn

EQUIPMENT
small saucepan   dry measures
knife   bowl
measuring spoons   spoon

- 2 tablespoons margarine *or* butter
- ¼ teaspoon ground cinnamon
- 4 cups popped popcorn
- 1 tablespoon presweetened cocoa powder

• In a small saucepan combine margarine or butter and cinnamon. Heat and stir till margarine is melted. Drizzle over popcorn; toss to mix. Sprinkle cocoa powder over top; toss again. Serve right away. Makes 4 cups.

Test your knowledge with this "pop" quiz. Guess true or false for each one.
- Ancient Indians used to think a little demon inside the corn kernels made them pop.
- The English colonists had popcorn at the first Thanksgiving dinner.
- Families in colonial times ate popcorn with sugar and cream as a breakfast cereal.
- Americans consume 9.9 billion quarts of popped popcorn every year.

Nothing corny about this quiz—they're all true! Now, reward yourself with a bowl of popcorn.

The Tops In "Pops"

Keep plenty of popped corn ready to munch for healthy by-the-handful snacking. Before you begin, make sure you know how to use your popcorn popper safely. When you're done making a batch of popcorn, store it in an airtight container. Then, simply dig in the next time you need a fix-it-fast snack.

Veggie Pickpockets

EQUIPMENT
knife cutting board
measuring spoons

2 small pita bread rounds
2 to 4 tablespoons creamy bacon salad dressing *or* any creamy salad dressing
8 thin cucumber slices
1 small carrot, thinly sliced

● Cut pitas in half. Open pockets. Generously spread inside of *each* half with salad dressing. Arrange *2* cucumber slices and *several* carrot slices in each pita half. Makes 2 to 4 servings.

Pita bread, also known as pocket bread, makes the perfect edible holder. To make opening the pockets a little easier, place pita bread halves on a paper towel in the microwave oven. Micro-cook on 100% power (high) for 10 seconds. Remove and gently press open.

Very Berry Parfaits

EQUIPMENT
dry measures measuring spoons
spoon 2 small parfait
knife glasses

1 8-ounce carton strawberry, raspberry, *or* blueberry yogurt
½ cup sliced strawberries, raspberries, *or* blueberries

● Spoon about *¼ cup* yogurt into 2 small parfait glasses. Spoon about *2 tablespoons* fruit into each glass. Spoon remaining yogurt into glasses. Top with remaining fruit. Makes 2 servings.

A terrific team of yogurt and fresh fruit makes this snack impossible to resist. It's the berries!

Triple Dream Shake

EQUIPMENT
blender knife
liquid measure measuring spoons

½ cup orange juice
½ of a medium banana, cut up
2 or 3 ice cubes
1 tablespoon nonfat dry milk powder

● In a blender container combine orange juice, banana, ice cubes, and dry milk. Cover and blend till mixed. Serve right away. Makes 1 serving.

Cranberry Catch: Prepare as directed above, *except* substitute ½ cup *cranberry juice cocktail* for orange juice.

Pep Rally Pineapple Shake: Prepare as directed above, *except* substitute ½ cup unsweetened *pineapple juice* for orange juice. If you like, sprinkle with toasted *coconut*.

Dreaming of a fruity thirst quencher after a long day of reading, writing, and 'rithmetic? Choose orange, cranberry, or pineapple to make your favorite flavor fantasy come true.

Tomato Tune-Up

EQUIPMENT
small saucepan liquid measure
spoon mug

1 6-ounce can tomato juice
¼ cup lemonade

● In a small saucepan combine tomato juice and lemonade. Bring to boiling. Pour into a mug. Makes 1 serving.

Microwave Directions: In a large microwave-safe mug stir together tomato juice and lemonade. Micro-cook on 100% power (high) for 2 to 3 minutes or till heated through.

After a tough workout on the courts or field, you need to recharge yourself. Start by transforming this sassy drink into a real thirst quencher. Just combine chilled tomato juice and lemonade and serve over ice.

Chocolate-Banana Fizz

EQUIPMENT
knife
ice cream scoop
liquid measure
blender
rubber spatula

Teen taster Carrie described this drink as "chocolate sauce over bananas." And that's exactly what it is—we just added a little fizz.

- 1 medium banana
- 2 large scoops vanilla ice cream (about 1 cup)
- ½ cup club soda
- ¼ cup chocolate-flavored syrup

● Peel banana and cut into large pieces. In a blender container combine all of the ingredients. Cover and blend till smooth. Serve right away. Makes 2 servings.

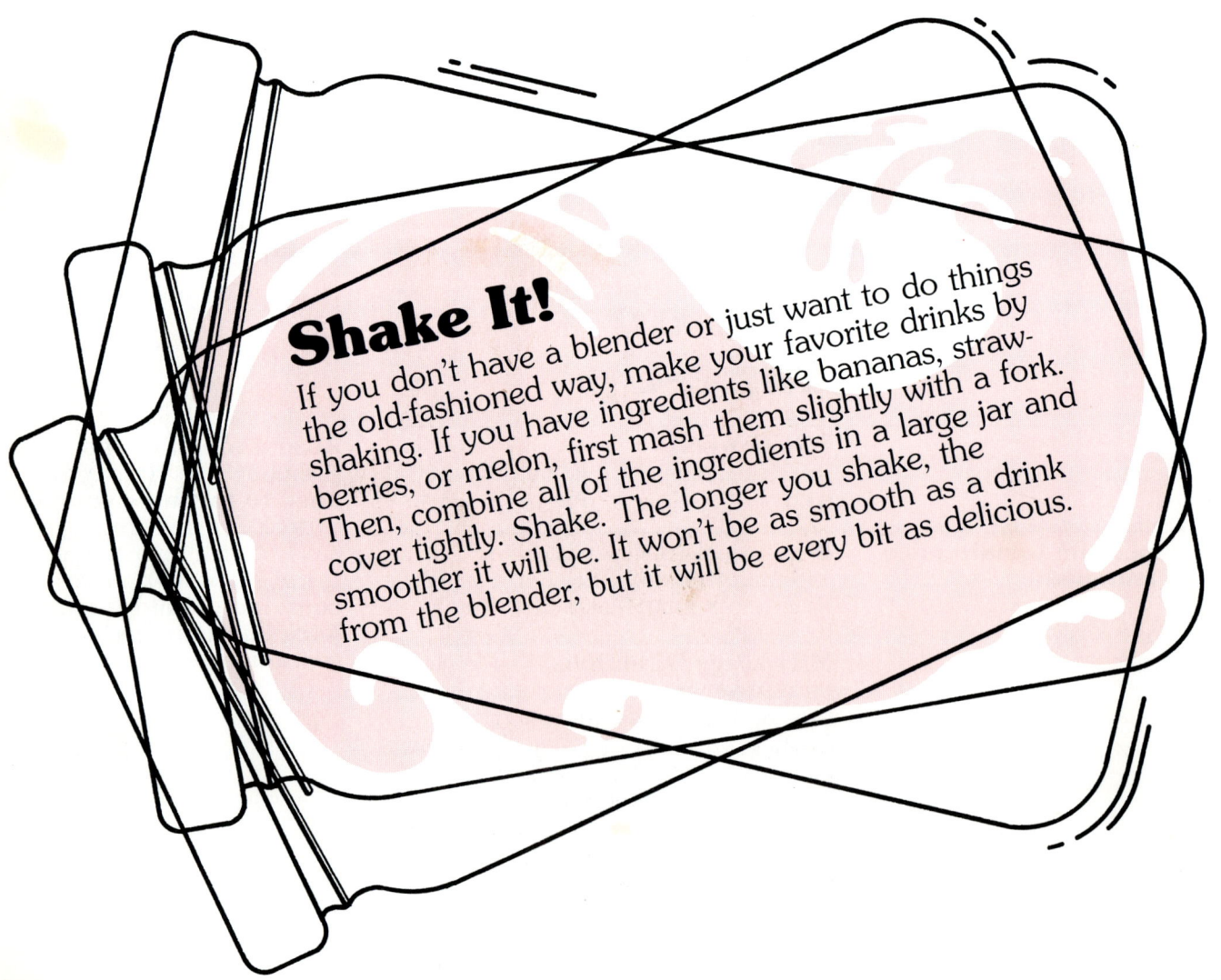

Shake It!

If you don't have a blender or just want to do things the old-fashioned way, make your favorite drinks by shaking. If you have ingredients like bananas, strawberries, or melon, first mash them slightly with a fork. Then, combine all of the ingredients in a large jar and cover tightly. Shake. The longer you shake, the smoother it will be. It won't be as smooth as a drink from the blender, but it will be every bit as delicious.

Cocoa Loco

EQUIPMENT
medium saucepan
measuring spoons
wooden spoon
liquid measure
rotary beater
ladle
mugs

This minty chocolate drink will make you loco for this hot cocoa!

3 tablespoons sugar
3 tablespoons unsweetened cocoa powder
¼ cup water

● In a medium saucepan stir together sugar and cocoa powder. Slowly stir in water. Cook over medium heat till mixture boils. Boil gently for 1 minute, stirring constantly.

1¾ cups milk
Few drops peppermint *or* orange extract
Peppermint *or* cinnamon sticks (optional)

● Slowly add milk, stirring as you add. Cook and stir till mixture starts to bubble around the edge of pan. Remove from heat. Stir in peppermint or orange extract. Using a rotary beater, beat till foamy. Ladle cocoa into mugs. Garnish with peppermint or cinnamon sticks, if you like. Makes 2 or 3 servings.

Firmly hold the rotary beater upright in the saucepan. Beat the cocoa until it's foamy and bubbly, as shown. It's important to keep the beater straight because tilting it can cause the hot cocoa to splash out of the pan.

Marvelous Melon Shake

EQUIPMENT
knife
melon baller
dry measure
blender
ice-cream scoop
liquid measure

A thick, creamy shake that's "one in a melon"!

| Watermelon, honeydew, *or* cantaloupe | ● Cut melon in half. Using a melon baller, scoop enough melon to measure ½ cup. Place in a blender container. |

| 2 large scoops vanilla ice cream (about 1 cup)
¼ cup milk | ● Add ice cream and milk. Cover and blend till smooth. Serve right away. Makes 1 serving. |

Yummy Yogurt Gulp

EQUIPMENT
blender
dry measures
liquid measure
measuring spoons

You can easily substitute fresh fruit for frozen in this tangy treat, but it won't be as cold.

½ cup frozen unsweetened strawberries, blueberries, *or* sliced peaches
½ cup vanilla yogurt
¼ cup milk
1 tablespoon toasted wheat germ
1 teaspoon sugar

● In a blender container combine all ingredients. Cover and blend till smooth. Serve right away. Makes 1 serving.

Never-Better Nachos

EQUIPMENT
15x10x1-inch baking pan
shredder
dry measures
hot pads
spoon

Spice up your nachos by replacing half of the cheddar cheese with Monterey Jack cheese with jalapeño peppers.

16 to 20 plain tortilla chips
1¼ cups shredded cheddar cheese
Chopped olives (optional)
Cooked bacon pieces (optional)
Sliced green onion (optional)
Dairy sour cream *or* taco sauce

● Spread tortilla chips in a single layer in a 15x10x1-inch baking pan. Sprinkle cheese over chips. Sprinkle with olives, bacon pieces, and green onion, if you like. Bake in a 400° oven for 2 to 3 minutes or till cheese melts. Transfer to a serving platter. Serve with sour cream or taco sauce. Makes 2 servings.

Microwave Directions: Arrange tortilla chips on a microwave-safe pizza plate; sprinkle cheese over chips. Sprinkle with olives, bacon, and onion. Micro-cook on 100% power (high) for 1 to 1½ minutes or till cheese melts.

Tangy Fruit Fluff

EQUIPMENT
small mixing bowl   spoon
dry measures   knife
measuring spoons   cutting board

¼ cup fruit-flavored yogurt
¼ cup frozen whipped dessert topping, thawed
1 teaspoon honey
  Coconut *or* sunflower nuts (optional)
  Desired fruit (see tip, right)

● In a small mixing bowl stir together yogurt, whipped dessert topping, and honey. Sprinkle with coconut or sunflower nuts, if you like. Dip fruits into mixture. Makes 2 servings.

Have we got some fruity suggestions for you to sink your teeth into! Use grapes, banana slices, apple or pear slices, cubed melon, or whole strawberries to dunk into this light, tangy dip.

Dandy Candy Whirl

EQUIPMENT
dry measures   ice-cream scoop
blender *or* food   rubber spatula
  processor

¼ cup broken chocolate-covered English toffee bar, chocolate-covered peanut butter cups, malted milk balls, *or* cream-filled chocolate cookies
1 pint vanilla ice cream, softened

● Place broken candy or chocolate cookies, then ice cream, in a blender container or food processor bowl. Cover and blend or process. Stop blender or food processor. Scrape down sides with a rubber spatula, if necessary. Cover and blend or process till well mixed. Serve right away. Makes 2 servings.

While you're breaking up the candy or cookies, let the ice cream stand at room temperature. This softens it, making it super-easy to scoop.

Quesadillas

EQUIPMENT
shredder
dry measures
knife
cutting board
measuring spoons
medium skillet
pancake turner
spoon

Olé! The idea for these quick cheese turnovers came from Mexico, our neighbor south of the border.

⅓ cup shredded Monterey Jack, cheddar, *or* Swiss cheese
1 8-inch flour tortilla
1 tablespoon chopped green pepper *or* tomato

● Sprinkle cheese on *half* of the tortilla. Top with green pepper or tomato. Fold in half, pressing down gently.

Salsa (optional)

● Heat a medium skillet over medium-high heat. Cook tortilla in skillet about 3 minutes, turning once (see photo, below). Cut quesadilla into 3 triangles. Serve with salsa, if you like. Makes 1 serving.

Using a pancake turner, carefully turn the quesadilla over. Make sure you turn it about halfway through the cooking time so the cheese melts evenly.

Ham and Cheddar Horns

If this recipe is music to your ears, you can sound an even easier note by substituting purchased cooked bacon pieces for the ham.

EQUIPMENT
baking sheet
knife
shredder
dry measures
cutting board
measuring spoons
hot pads
metal spatula

1 package (4) refrigerated crescent rolls
Prepared mustard

- Unroll crescent rolls. Tear along perforations. Place 4 triangles on an ungreased baking sheet. Spread lightly with mustard.

¼ cup shredded cheddar cheese
¼ cup finely chopped fully cooked ham

- Sprinkle *each* with 1 tablespoon cheese and 1 tablespoon cooked ham. Starting at large end, roll dough toward point. Fold ends in slightly to form "horns." Bake in a 375° oven for 11 to 13 minutes or till golden. Serves 4.

Salad On a Bun

EQUIPMENT
bread knife
cutting board
small bowl
measuring spoons
spoon
knife

2 club rolls
3 tablespoons mayonnaise *or* salad dressing
1 tablespoon bottled barbecue sauce
1 tablespoon cooked bacon *or* ham pieces

● Cut rolls in half horizontally. In a small bowl stir together mayonnaise or salad dressing, barbecue sauce, and bacon or ham pieces. Spread about *1 tablespoon* mixture on each roll half.

Lettuce leaves
2 slices tomato
4 slices cucumber
2 rings green pepper

● On bottom halves of rolls, place lettuce. Top with tomato, cucumber, and green pepper. Replace tops, cut side down. Makes 2 servings.

Case of the Dual Identity. As Vic begins preparing his after-school snack, it becomes clear this is no ordinary snack. The crunch and munch of fresh vegetables make it a salad, but the fresh roll and snappy spread make it a sandwich. Only you can solve this mystery. You'll find the answer in the taste. Have a bite and decide: Is it a sandwich, or a salad, or both?

23 Make-the-Grade Munchies

Fruit Kabobs

EQUIPMENT
knife
cutting board
small bowl
spoon
small saucepan
dry measures
can opener
strainer
4 metal skewers
broiler pan *or* baking sheet
pastry brush
hot pads

Sherrie, one of our tasters, suggested threading bananas or cherries on the kabobs for a different taste. Have fun experimenting with your favorite fruits. Just make sure the fruit pieces are about the same size so everything cooks evenly.

1 small apple 1 small pear Lemon juice	● Core apple and pear. Cut each quarter crosswise in half. Toss apple and pear pieces with lemon juice.
¼ cup orange marmalade *or* pineapple preserves	● In a small saucepan heat orange marmalade or pineapple preserves over medium heat just till melted.
1 8¼-ounce can pineapple chunks, drained	● Alternate apple, pear, and pineapple chunks on 4 metal skewers. Place skewers on a broiler pan or baking sheet. Brush with marmalade or preserves. Broil fruit 4 inches from the heat for 6 to 8 minutes or till heated through and slightly tender; turning once. Serves 4.

To core the apple or pear, cut it in half. Cut the fruit in half again. Place one quarter, flat side down, on the cutting board. Cut down along the core, as shown.

Orange-Pineapple Fruit Dip

EQUIPMENT
small bowl
spoon *or* rubber spatula
wire whisk *or* rotary beater
cutting board
knife

Light and fluffy and slightly sweet, this concoction makes a delightful dip.

1 8-ounce carton orange yogurt
½ of an 8-ounce container soft-style cream cheese with pineapple
2 tablespoons sugar

• In a small bowl stir together yogurt, cream cheese, and sugar. Using a wire whisk or rotary beater, beat till smooth.

Strawberries, seedless grapes, cherries, apple slices, pear slices, *or* pineapple wedges

• If necessary, cut up desired fruit. Serve dip with fruit. Cover and chill leftover dip. Makes 1½ cups dip.

Cheese Wheels

EQUIPMENT
knife   measuring spoons

Looking for fun flavor combinations? Try these:
- Ham and soft-style cream cheese with pineapple
- Roast beef and cream cheese with chives
- Roast beef and whipped cream cheese with bacon and horseradish
- Turkey and soft-style cream cheese with toasted-onion

2 thin slices fully cooked ham, roast beef, *or* turkey
4 teaspoons cream cheese

• Spread each slice of ham, roast beef, or turkey with about *2 teaspoons* cream cheese. Starting at short end, roll up. Cut into 2-inch pieces. Makes 1 serving.

Jam and Biscuits

EQUIPMENT
kitchen scissors   measuring spoons
baking sheet   hot pads

1 package (10) refrigerated biscuits
5 teaspoons jam *or* jelly

Separate biscuits.

Use kitchen scissors to make 5 short cuts around the edge of each biscuit. Do not cut all the way to center. Place on a baking sheet.

Press your fingers in the center of each biscuit to make a dent.

Spoon about ½ teaspoon jam or jelly into indentation.

Bake in a 450° oven for 8 to 10 minutes or till golden. Serve warm. Makes 10.

Rosy-Posy Applesauce

EQUIPMENT
medium saucepan measuring spoons
can opener wooden spoon

1 15-ounce jar applesauce
1 8-ounce can whole cranberry sauce
⅛ teaspoon ground nutmeg
⅛ teaspoon ground cinnamon

● In a medium saucepan stir together all ingredients. Cook and stir over medium heat about 5 minutes or till heated through. Makes 4 servings.

Want this fruity snack cold? Before you leave for school in the morning, place the applesauce and cranberry sauce in the refrigerator. Then, when the hungries hit, just stir together the ingredients.

Microwave Directions: In a medium microwave-safe bowl stir together all ingredients. Cover with plastic wrap, leaving a small area uncovered. Micro-cook on 100% power (high) for 5 to 6 minutes or till heated through.

Sugar-and-Spice Twirls

EQUIPMENT
2 pie plates knife
dry measures small saucepan
measuring spoons muffin pans
spoon hot pads

½ cup sugar
1½ teaspoons ground cinnamon
1 package (8) refrigerated breadsticks

● In a pie plate stir together sugar and cinnamon. Set aside. Separate breadsticks. Halve each breadstick.

Made of sugar and spice and everything nice, these tasty twirls were a favorite with our teen tasters.

3 tablespoons margarine *or* butter

● In a small saucepan melt margarine or butter; pour into a separate pie plate.
 Dip each breadstick into margarine or butter, then roll each in sugar-cinnamon mixture to coat. Coil each rope in the bottom of a muffin pan. Bake in a 425° oven for 10 to 12 minutes or till light brown. Makes 16 twirls.

27 Make-the-Grade Munchies

Mighty Apricot Muffins

EQUIPMENT
muffin pans
paper bake cups
medium mixing bowl
dry measures
measuring spoons
wooden spoon
fork
small bowl
liquid measure
kitchen scissors
hot pads
small mixing bowl

Jazz up biscuits or toast with leftover Apricot Spread.

1¼ cups whole wheat flour
½ cup wheat germ
½ cup quick-cooking rolled oats
2 teaspoons baking powder
¼ teaspoon salt

● Line muffin pans with paper bake cups; set aside. In a medium mixing bowl stir together flour, wheat germ, oats, baking powder, and salt.

1 slightly beaten egg
½ cup apricot nectar
½ cup milk
¼ cup honey
2 tablespoons cooking oil

● Add egg, apricot nectar, milk, honey, and cooking oil; stir just till moistened.

½ cup dried apricots
⅓ cup chopped nuts (optional)
Apricot Spread

● Using kitchen scissors, snip apricots. Stir apricots into batter. If you like, stir in nuts. Fill muffin pans *two-thirds* full. Bake in a 400° oven about 15 minutes. Serve with Apricot Spread. Makes 12.

Apricot Spread: In a small mixing bowl stir together ½ cup *margarine or butter,* softened, and 2 tablespoons *apricot preserves.* Cover and chill.

Scrambled Sandwich

EQUIPMENT
knife
cutting board
small bowl
measuring spoons
wire whisk *or*
  rotary beater
6-inch skillet
shredder
dry measures
wooden spoon

A nutritious, delicious snack, this scrambled egg sandwich is a perfect way to start the day, too. In less than 15 minutes you can have it ready to go.

1 pita bread round 2 tomato slices 2 eggs 1 tablespoon milk Dash pepper	● Cut pita bread in half. Open pockets. Place 1 tomato slice in each pita bread half. In a small bowl beat together eggs, milk, and pepper.
2 teaspoons margarine *or* butter	● In a 6-inch skillet melt margarine or butter. Pour egg mixture into skillet. Cook over medium heat for 1 minute, without stirring.
¼ cup shredded cheddar *or* Monterey Jack cheese with jalapeño peppers 1 tablespoon cooked bacon pieces	● Sprinkle with cheese and bacon pieces. Using a wooden spoon, stir egg mixture. Continue cooking over medium heat about 2 minutes or till eggs are cooked, but still moist (see photo, below). Spoon eggs into pita bread halves. Makes 2 servings.

As the eggs cook, stir occasionally. Stirring too often breaks the eggs up too much. When done, the eggs should still look moist, as shown.

Sweet 'n' Sour Bites

EQUIPMENT
medium saucepan
knife
dry measures
measuring spoons
spoon

1 5½-ounce package small smoked sausage links *or* 3 hot dogs, cut into bite-size pieces
¼ cup apple jelly
1 teaspoon vinegar
1 teaspoon soy sauce
1 teaspoon prepared mustard

● In a medium saucepan stir together all ingredients. Cook and stir over medium-high heat till boiling. Boil for 2 minutes more or till sauce is slightly thickened. Makes 2 or 3 servings.

The sweet comes from the apple jelly; the sour, from the vinegar.

Fruit Stack-Ups

EQUIPMENT
knife
cutting board
measuring spoons
2 small bowls
wooden toothpicks

1 small banana
1 small apple *or* pear
2 tablespoons orange juice

● Peel banana and cut into bite-size pieces. Core apple or pear and cut into bite-size pieces. In a small bowl toss together banana, apple or pear, and orange juice together.

Strawberries, grapes, melon cubes *or* balls, *or* pineapple chunks

● Thread pieces of banana, apple or pear, and other desired fruit onto wooden toothpicks, using 2 or 3 pieces for each stack-up.

½ of a 4-ounce container soft-style cream cheese with pineapple *or* strawberry
2 to 3 tablespoons milk

● In a small bowl combine cream cheese and enough milk to make of dipping consistency. Dip fruit into sauce. Cover and chill any leftover sauce. Makes 2 servings.

If stacking and dunking aren't your style, pile the fruit in a bowl. Drizzle the cream cheese sauce over the fruit and eat the fruit with a spoon.

Wonderful Wafflewich: Toast 2 *frozen waffles* according to package directions. Spread *1* waffle with 1 tablespoon *peanut butter*. Arrange 1 small *banana, sliced,* on top of peanut butter. Top with second waffle. Cut in half. Makes 1 serving.

Sugar-and-Spice Waffles: Combine 1 teaspoon *sugar* and 1/8 teaspoon ground *cinnamon*. Toast 2 *frozen waffles* according to package directions. Sprinkle sugar mixture over waffles. Squirt *pressurized dessert topping* on waffles. Sprinkle with chopped *pecans*. Serves 2.

Pie à la Mode Waffles *(Also pictured on the cover.):* Toast 2 *frozen waffles* according to package directions. Meanwhile, heat 1/2 cup fruit *pie filling* in a small saucepan till warm. Place some *ice cream* on each waffle. Spoon pie filling over ice cream. Makes 2 servings.

Yo-Go Waffles: Toast *frozen waffles* according to package directions. Dollop waffles with *vanilla or fruit-flavored yogurt*. Sprinkle with chopped *fruit* and chopped *nuts*. Makes 2 servings.

Winning Waffles

Cheesy Bagelwich

EQUIPMENT
small mixing bowl
measuring spoons
shredder
spoon
bread knife
cutting board
knife

Bagels are a traditional Jewish bread. Although bagels taste like a chewy dinner roll, they look more like a doughnut.

| 2 tablespoons dairy sour cream
2 tablespoons shredded carrot
1 teaspoon snipped chives *or* parsley
½ teaspoon Dijon-style mustard | ● In a small mixing bowl stir together sour cream, carrot, chives, and mustard. |

| 2 bagels
Lettuce
2 slices Monterey Jack, mozzarella, *or* cheddar cheese
1 small tomato, sliced | ● Slice bagels in half. Spread bottom half of bagels with sour cream mixture. Top with lettuce, cheese, and tomato. Top with remaining bagel half. Serves 2. |

Confetti Spread

EQUIPMENT
small mixing bowl
dry measures
shredder
measuring spoons
spoon
knife

Experiment! Try this colorful spread as a sandwich, on carrot or celery sticks, or on apple or pear wedges.

| ⅓ cup cottage cheese
1 tablespoon shredded carrot *or* zucchini
1 tablespoon chopped nuts
1 tablespoon dairy sour cream *or* mayonnaise | ● In a small bowl stir together cottage cheese, carrot or zucchini, nuts, and sour cream or mayonnaise. |

| Crackers, pita triangles, bagels, *or* bread | ● Spread cottage cheese mixture on crackers, pita triangles, bagels, or bread. Makes 1 or 2 servings. |

Cheesewiches

EQUIPMENT
medium skillet
knife
shredder
dry measures
measuring spoons
pancake turner
plate

A winner among our teen testers and tasters, no one had a problem "building" or "demolishing" these grilled sandwiches.

1 tablespoon margarine *or* butter
4 slices bread
4 slices American *or* Swiss cheese
¼ cup shredded carrot *or* 1 small apple, cored and thinly sliced
2 tablespoons sunflower nuts

- In a medium skillet melt margarine or butter. Top *2* slices of bread with a slice of cheese. Top with carrot or apple, then sunflower nuts. Top with remaining cheese slices, then bread slices. Carefully place in skillet.

- Cook over medium-low heat for 5 to 7 minutes or till bottom is golden brown. Using a pancake turner, carefully turn each sandwich. Cook on the other side about 2 minutes or till golden brown. Transfer to a plate. Cut each cheesewich into 4 triangles. Makes 4 servings.

Make It Micro!

When going solo on the snack and supper scene, you want to make it as easy, safe, and speedy as possible. Using your microwave is the perfect way to move things along. Just be sure you know how it works. Here are a couple of hints to help you.

- Use only microwave-safe containers. (Try storing them together in a special place.)
- Micro-cook snacks on paper plates, towels, or napkins. Use only those paper products labeled "microwave-safe."
- Always use hot pads when removing containers from the microwave. Hot food can make utensils hot.
- Remember, small amounts of food cook faster than larger amounts. So, heating one mug of cocoa will take less time than two mugs.
- Frozen foods take longer to cook than foods that are chilled or thawed.
- Follow package directions carefully when micro-cooking frozen foods.

Pumpkin-Pie Party Mix

EQUIPMENT
8x8x2-inch baking pan
dry measures
wooden spoon
small saucepan
knife
measuring spoons
hot pads
cooling rack
airtight container

If only "Peter, Peter, pumpkin eater" were around to enjoy this crunchy mix. Cereal, chow mein noodles, and pecans are tossed with a honey and pumpkin pie spice mixture and then lightly toasted. Any "pumpkin eater" would approve!

1¼ cups crispy corn and rice square cereal
⅓ cup chow mein noodles
⅓ cup broken pecans

- In an 8x8x2-inch baking pan stir together corn and rice cereal, chow mein noodles, and pecans.

2 tablespoons margarine *or* butter
2 teaspoons honey
½ teaspoon pumpkin pie spice

- In a small saucepan stir together margarine or butter, honey, and pumpkin pie spice. Heat and stir mixture till margarine is melted. Drizzle over cereal mixture; toss to mix.

- Bake in a 350° oven about 12 minutes, stirring once. Cool in pan on a cooling rack. Store in an airtight container. Makes 2 cups.

Microwave Directions: In a 1½-quart casserole combine corn and rice cereal, chow mein noodles, and pecans. In a 1-cup measure combine margarine or butter, honey, and pumpkin pie spice. Micro-cook, uncovered, on 100% power (high) for 30 to 60 seconds or till margarine is melted. Stir. Pour mixture over cereal mixture; toss to mix. Micro-cook, uncovered, on 100% power (high) for 2½ minutes, stirring twice during cooking. Cool, stirring occasionally. (Mix will crisp as it stands.)

34 Twice-As-Nice Nibbles

2 TREATS IN 1

Double your fun with half the work! These recipes use similar (or the same) ingredients to give you two delightfully *different* snacks. Make both right now—eat one, and save the other for later.

2 TREATS IN 1

Chocolate Chippers

Sandwich your favorite flavor of ice cream or sherbet between these oh-so-good cookies.

EQUIPMENT	
medium bowl	spoon
dry measures	cookie sheet
measuring spoons	hot pads
wooden spoon	pancake turner
small mixer bowl	cooling rack
electric mixer	ice-cream scoop
knife	plastic wrap

1¼ cups all-purpose flour ½ teaspoon baking soda	In a medium bowl stir together flour and baking soda.
½ cup margarine *or* butter ½ cup packed brown sugar ¼ cup sugar	In a mixer bowl beat margarine with an electric mixer on medium speed for 30 seconds. Add sugars; beat till fluffy.
1 egg ¾ teaspoon vanilla 1 cup miniature *or* regular semisweet chocolate pieces	Add egg and vanilla; beat well. Add dry ingredients to mixture, beating till well combined. Stir in chocolate pieces.
	Drop dough from a rounded teaspoon 2 inches apart onto an ungreased cookie sheet. Bake in a 375° oven for 8 to 10 minutes. Cool about 1 minute on cookie sheet. Transfer to a cooling rack; cool completely. Set aside some cookies for cookie sandwiches. Makes 36.
Ice cream *or* sherbet	For each cookie sandwich, place a small scoop of ice cream on the flat side of 1 cookie; top with a second cookie. Wrap in plastic wrap. Seal with tape. Freeze.

Peachy Keen Slush

EQUIPMENT
blender
liquid measure
dry measures
rubber spatula
glasses
shallow pan
spoon

The slush will become thicker as you add the ice cubes, so you may need to stop the blender once or twice and stir the mixture.

½ of a 16-ounce package frozen unsweetened peach slices (2 cups) 1 cup orange juice ¼ cup frozen lemonade concentrate ¼ cup water	In a blender container combine frozen peach slices, orange juice, lemonade concentrate, and water. Cover and blend till mixture is smooth.
5 ice cubes	With the blender running, add ice cubes, one at a time, through hole in lid. Stop machine. Scrape down sides with a rubber spatula, if necessary. Pour desired amount into glasses. Serve right away.
	For peach ice, place remaining mixture in a shallow pan. Cover and freeze overnight or till frozen. Let stand at room temperature for 10 minutes. Scrape with a spoon to serve. Makes about 3 cups.
	Berry Bash: Prepare as directed above, *except* substitute 2 cups unsweetened *whole strawberries or* unsweetened *raspberries* for peaches. Add 2 tablespoons sifted *powdered sugar*.

37 Twice-As-Nice Nibbles

Tangy Fruit Tempters

EQUIPMENT
blender
ice-cream scoop
liquid measure
glasses
small paper cups
aluminum foil
knife
wooden sticks

No cutting, no chopping, no coring, no peeling—just dump the frozen mixed fruit into the blender with the ice cream and buttermilk. How easy can it be!

1 10-ounce package frozen mixed fruit in quick-thaw pouch
1 pint vanilla ice cream
1 cup buttermilk

In a blender container combine frozen mixed fruit, ice cream, and buttermilk. Cover and blend till smooth and frothy. Pour desired amount into glasses. Serve right away.

For frozen pops, divide remaining mixture between small paper cups. Cover each cup with foil. Make a small hole in the foil with a knife. Insert a wooden stick through the hole in center of cup. Freeze overnight. Remove foil and peel off paper cups. Makes about 3 cups.

CC Shake

EQUIPMENT
blender
liquid measure
ice-cream scoop
can opener
dry measure
rubber spatula
glasses
small paper cups
aluminum foil
knife
wooden sticks

One "C" stands for cranberry. Cranberry sauce and whole cranberries go into this double-delicious shake. The other "C" is for cream cheese. Just one package makes it thick and rich and smooth—so good it rivals cheesecake.

1 egg
1 3-ounce package cream cheese, softened
½ cup milk
4 large scoops vanilla ice cream (2 cups)
1 8-ounce can jellied cranberry sauce
1 cup cranberries

Place egg in a blender container. Cover and blend for 15 to 30 seconds. Add cream cheese and milk. Cover and blend till well combined. Add ice cream, cranberry sauce, and cranberries. Stop and scrape down sides, if necessary. Pour desired amount into glasses. Serve right away.

For frozen pops, divide remaining mixture among small paper cups. Cover each cup with foil. Make a small hole in the foil with a knife. Insert a wooden stick through the hole in center of cup. Freeze overnight. Remove foil and peel off paper cups. Makes about 4 cups.

Mucho-Gusto Munchies

- 2 cups shredded lettuce
- 1 9-ounce can bean dip
- ⅔ cup sour cream dip with chives
- 1 small tomato, chopped
- ½ cup shredded cheddar cheese
- ½ cup sliced black olives
- Corn chips

Line a salad plate with *half* of the lettuce. Spoon bean dip on lettuce. Spread *half* of the sour cream dip over bean dip. Sprinkle with *half* of the tomato, *half* of the cheese, and *half* of the olives. Serve with corn chips. Makes 2 to 4 servings.

EQUIPMENT
salad plate
spoon
knife
cutting board
dry measures
measuring spoons
shredder
plastic wrap

2 TREATS IN 1

1 3-ounce can deviled ham
2 6-inch flour tortillas *or* 2 taco shells

For roll-ups, evenly divide deviled ham and remaining sour cream dip between tortillas or taco shells. Sprinkle remaining lettuce, tomato, cheese, and olives on top. Roll up each tortilla. Wrap in plastic wrap; chill. Makes 2 servings.

PB&J Shake And Shiver

EQUIPMENT
blender
liquid measure
ice-cream scoop
dry measures
measuring spoons
glasses
muffin pan
paper bake cups

In addition to peanut butter (PB) and jelly (J), this thick, frosty shake has chocolate milk and vanilla ice cream. Now that's a treat!

2 cups chocolate milk
2 large scoops vanilla ice cream (1 cup)
½ cup peanut butter
2 tablespoons jelly

In a blender container combine chocolate milk, ice cream, peanut butter, and jelly. Cover; blend till smooth. Pour desired amount into glasses. Serve right away.

Chocolate sauce (optional)
Chopped peanuts (optional)

For frozen treats, line muffin pan with paper bake cups. Divide remaining mixture among muffin cups. Freeze till firm. Remove frozen mixture from paper bake cups. Serve with chocolate sauce and chopped peanuts, if you like. Makes about 3½ cups.

Tropical Teasers

EQUIPMENT
small saucepan
knife
large bowl
dry measures
measuring spoons
wooden spoon
can opener
strainer
medium mixing bowl
liquid measure
6-ounce custard cups
clear plastic wrap

Aloha! Tropical coconut, banana, and pineapple make this pair of popcorn and pudding snacks a scrumptious South Seas sensation.

3 tablespoons margarine *or* butter
4 cups popped popcorn
1 4-serving-size package *instant* coconut *or* banana cream pudding mix

In a small saucepan heat margarine or butter till melted. In a large bowl combine popcorn, melted margarine, and *3 tablespoons* of *dry* pudding mix. Toss to coat. Serve right away.

1 8-ounce can crushed pineapple (juice pack)
1 small banana
1½ cups milk

Drain pineapple. Peel and slice banana. Set aside. In a mixing bowl combine milk and remaining *dry* pudding mix according to package directions. Stir in pineapple and banana. Divide mixture among four 6-ounce custard cups. Cover and chill. Makes 4 servings.

41 Twice-As-Nice Nibbles

Ice Cream And Candy

EQUIPMENT
medium mixing bowl
can opener
liquid measure
dry measures
measuring spoons
airtight container
large mixer bowl
electric mixer
wooden spoon
8x8x2-inch baking pan
aluminum foil
serving bowls

Ice cream that's a dream and candy that's dandy! From a single can of sweetened condensed milk you get two deliciously sweet treats.

1 14-ounce can (1⅓ cups) *sweetened condensed* milk ½ cup peanut butter 1½ cups granola	In a medium mixing bowl combine *half* of the sweetened condensed milk and peanut butter. Stir in granola. Using *1 tablespoon* of mixture shape into balls. Place candy in an airtight container. Store, covered, in the refrigerator. Makes 25 balls.
1 pint whipping cream (2 cups) ½ teaspoon vanilla extract	In a large mixer bowl combine remaining sweetened condensed milk, whipping cream, and vanilla. Chill for 30 minutes. Beat with an electric mixer on high speed till soft peaks form.
12 gingersnaps, chocolate-covered graham crackers, chocolate wafers, macaroons, *or* sandwich cookies	Coarsely crumble cookies; fold into cream mixture. Transfer to an 8x8x2-inch pan. Cover with foil and freeze overnight. To serve, scoop into serving bowls. Makes about 5 cups.

Using your hands, shape about 1 tablespoon of granola mixture into balls.

Beat whipping cream and evaporated milk till soft peaks form. To see if peaks have formed, lift the beaters from the bowl, as shown.

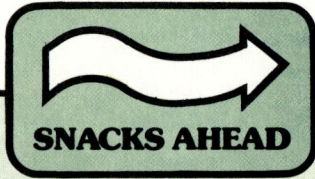

SNACKS AHEAD

Plan ahead for your after-class snacks, so you'll have goodies on hand when you get home. Spend a few minutes making these tasty treats the night before or in the morning before school. Watch out though: these make-ahead marvels are so delicious you'll be tempted to eat them right away!

Space Shake

EQUIPMENT
blender
ice cream scoop
can opener
liquid measure
9x5x3-inch loaf pan *or* 1-quart freezer container
aluminum foil

We call this treat a Space Shake because it has an out-of-this-world taste. Fresh, fruity, full of flavor, this creamy drink can be made for one, two, three, or four snackers.

6 large scoops vanilla ice cream (about 3 cups)
1 8-ounce can crushed pineapple (juice pack)
½ cup milk

● In a blender container place ice cream, *undrained* pineapple, and milk. Cover and blend till mixture is smooth. Pour mixture into a 9x5x3-inch loaf pan or a 1-quart freezer container. Cover with foil and freeze.

1 cup milk

● Before serving, let ice cream mixture stand at room temperature about 10 minutes. Scoop mixture into a blender container. Add milk. (For each serving, scoop ¼ of the frozen mixture. Add ¼ of the milk). Cover and blend just till smooth. Serve right away. Serves 4.

Peanut-Chocolate Shake: Prepare shake as directed above, *except* substitute *chocolate ice cream* for the vanilla ice cream, ¼ cup creamy *peanut butter* for crushed pineapple, and ¾ cup milk for the ½ cup milk.

Great Grape Fruit Pops

EQUIPMENT
can opener
liquid measure
pitcher
spoon
paper cups
aluminum foil
knife
wooden sticks

2 cups unsweetened grape juice
1½ cups cold water
1 6-ounce can frozen pink lemonade concentrate

● In a pitcher combine all ingredients. Stir till mixed. Pour into twelve 3-ounce paper cups. Cover *each* cup with foil. Make a small hole in the center of the foil with a knife. Insert a wooden stick through the hole. Freeze for 6 hours or till firm. Remove from the freezer 5 minutes before serving. Remove foil and peel paper cups from pops. Makes 12.

Turn your tastebuds loose with these frosty grape and lemonade pops. Make them the night before. Then, five minutes after you walk in the door, you'll be ready to enjoy. Pucker up!

Anytime Snowballs

EQUIPMENT
dry measures
knife
cutting board
small bowl
spoon
ice-cream scoop
freezerproof dishes

Ice cream *or* sherbet
¼ cup cashews *or* peanuts
¼ cup coconut

● Remove ice cream from freezer. Meanwhile, chop nuts. In a small bowl stir together nuts and coconut.

● Scoop 1 ball of ice cream or sherbet. Drop into nut-coconut mixture. Roll ice cream until coated with nut mixture, pressing mixture onto ice cream with fingers. Repeat with another scoop. Place in freezerproof dishes. Cover and freeze till firm. Makes 2 servings.

We call them "anytime" because it doesn't have to be snowing to make—or eat—these frosty treats.

44 Make-Ahead Teasers, After-School Pleasers

Crush *half* of the crackers at a time into fine crumbs.

Pat the cracker-margarine mixture evenly over the bottom of the pan.

Spread the pudding mixture on top.

Spoon cherries over the pudding mixture.

Pudding Pie Squares

EQUIPMENT	
plastic bag	small mixer bowl
rolling pin	liquid measure
8x8x2-inch baking dish	electric mixer
small saucepan	rubber spatula
fork	can opener
knife	spoon
	clear plastic wrap

Three cheers for *Pudding Pie Squares!* So cool and creamy, so rich and dreamy. For something else to cheer about, try different flavored pudding mixes and pie fillings. For a twist try combining vanilla and cherries, lemon and blueberries, French vanilla and apricots, or banana cream and strawberries.

20 squares graham crackers	● Place *10* graham crackers in a plastic bag. Close bag. Using a rolling pin, crush crackers. Place in an 8x8x2-inch baking dish. Repeat with remaining crackers. Set aside *2 tablespoons* crumbs.
⅓ cup margarine *or* butter	● In a small saucepan melt margarine or butter over low heat. Pour into baking dish. Using a fork, stir together crackers and margarine. Using your hands, pat mixture evenly over bottom. Chill in the freezer for 10 minutes.
1 8-ounce carton dairy sour cream 1 package 4-serving-size *instant* chocolate *or* vanilla pudding mix 1 cup milk	● Meanwhile, place sour cream in a small mixer bowl. Add *dry* pudding mix and milk. Beat with an electric mixer on low speed about 1 minute. Turn mixer off. Using a rubber spatula, scrape sides of the bowl. Beat for 30 seconds more. Pour into dish; spread over crust.
1 21-ounce can cherry pie filling	● Carefully spoon pie filling over pudding mixture. Sprinkle with reserved crumbs. Cover the dish with clear plastic wrap. Chill for at least 3 hours or overnight. Cut into squares. Serves 9.

Butter Pecan Pudding

EQUIPMENT
dry measures
shallow baking pan
hot pads
liquid measure
mixing bowl
rotary beater
wooden spoon
6-ounce custard cups

½ cup chopped pecans	● Place pecans in a shallow baking pan. Bake in a 350° oven for 5 to 10 minutes. (*Or,* place pecans in a 9-inch microwave-safe pie plate. Micro-cook on 100% power (high) for 5 to 6 minutes.)
1½ cups milk ½ cup plain yogurt 1 4-serving-size package *instant* **butterscotch, chocolate,** *or* **vanilla pudding**	● In a mixing bowl combine milk and yogurt. Add *dry* pudding mix. Using a rotary beater, beat till smooth.
Frozen whipped dessert topping, thawed (optional)	● Stir in pecans. Pour into four 6-ounce custard cups. Cover and chill overnight. Top with whipped dessert topping, if you like. Makes 4 servings.

Some of our teen tasters who weren't so nuts about nuts suggested substituting chocolate chips. We thought it was a great idea. (It's less work too, because you get to skip the first step.)

Crunchy Peanut Butter Cookies

EQUIPMENT
- small bowl
- dry measures
- measuring spoons
- wooden spoon
- knife
- mixer bowl
- electric mixer
- cutting board
- clear plastic wrap *or* waxed paper
- ruler
- cookie sheet
- hot pads
- pancake turner
- cooling rack

Fresh-from-the-oven piping-hot cookies and a glass of icy-cold milk—the perfect after-school snack. Have these peanutty treats less than 15 minutes after you walk in the door. All you have to do is slice the make-ahead logs and bake.

1¼ cups all-purpose flour
½ teaspoon baking soda
⅛ teaspoon salt
¼ cup margarine *or* butter
½ cup peanut butter
⅓ cup sugar
⅓ cup packed brown sugar
1 egg
½ teaspoon vanilla

● In a small bowl stir together flour, soda, and salt. In a mixer bowl beat margarine or butter for 30 seconds. Add peanut butter, sugar, and brown sugar. Beat till fluffy. Add egg and vanilla and beat well. Add dry ingredients to beaten mixture, beating till well mixed.

⅓ cup peanuts

● Finely chop peanuts. Divide dough in half. Shape each portion of dough into a 7-inch log. Roll the dough in chopped peanuts to coat outside of logs. Wrap in clear plastic wrap or waxed paper. Chill for several hours or overnight.

● Cut dough into ¼-inch-thick slices. (Cut only as many slices as you need.) Rewrap remaining *unsliced* dough and return it to the refrigerator. Place cookie slices on an ungreased cookie sheet. Bake in a 375° oven for 8 to 10 minutes. Cool about 1 minute. Using a pancake turner, transfer cookies to a cooling rack. Makes about 48 cookies.

Frozen Banana Bites

EQUIPMENT
baking sheet
waxed paper
small saucepan
dry measures
wooden spoon
measuring spoons
knife
toothpicks
spoon

Bite-size bananas dipped in chocolate, rolled in crunchy brickle pieces, and frozen. An icy-cold tummy pleaser.

¼ cup semisweet chocolate pieces
¼ cup butterscotch pieces
2 teaspoons shortening

● Line a baking sheet with waxed paper. Set aside. In a small saucepan melt chocolate pieces and butterscotch pieces over *low* heat, stirring constantly. Stir in shortening. Remove from heat.

2 firm bananas
¾ cup almond brickle pieces, chopped nuts, *or* coconut

● Peel bananas and cut into bite-size pieces. Insert toothpicks into banana pieces. Sprinkle almond brickle pieces, nuts, or coconut on waxed paper.

● Using a spoon, drizzle chocolate-butterscotch mixture over banana pieces. Roll coated banana pieces in brickle pieces. Place on a baking sheet. Freeze till firm. Place in storage bags. Freeze. Makes 4 servings.

Spoon the coating over the banana pieces, turning the toothpick as you coat. Work over the saucepan so the extra coating falls into the pan.

Roll the coated banana in almond brickle pieces, nuts, or coconut until it's well coated.

Ham 'n' Cheddar Spread

EQUIPMENT
small mixing bowl
measuring spoons
wooden spoon
knife
cutting board
dry measures
shredder

Not one, but two kinds of cheese give this spread its smooth, creamy texture.

1 8-ounce container soft-style cream cheese with chives and onion
1 teaspoon prepared mustard

● In a small mixing bowl stir together cream cheese and mustard.

⅓ cup finely chopped fully cooked ham
¼ cup shredded cheddar cheese
Crackers, bread, *or* celery sticks

● Stir in ham and cheddar cheese. Cover and chill. Spread on crackers, bread, or celery sticks. Cover and store leftover spread in the refrigerator for up to 5 days. Makes 3 or 4 servings.

Beef 'n' Swiss Spread: Prepare spread as directed above, *except* substitute *cooked roast beef* for the ham and *Swiss cheese* for the cheddar.

Turkey 'n' Mozzarella Spread: Prepare spread as directed above, *except* substitute *cooked turkey* for the ham and *mozzarella cheese* for the cheddar.

Chili Skillet

EQUIPMENT
can opener
kitchen scissors
strainer
knife
cutting board
medium skillet
spoon
shredder

- 1 12½-ounce package (6) frozen corn muffins
- 1 7½-ounce can tomatoes *or* tomatoes with jalapeño peppers
- 1 7-ounce can whole kernel corn
- 1 15-ounce can chili with beans
- 1 medium onion, chopped
- 1 cup shredded Monterey Jack *or* Monterey Jack cheese with jalapeño peppers

● Remove 4 corn muffins from package to thaw. Using kitchen scissors, cut up tomatoes in can. Drain corn.

In a medium skillet combine chili, *undrained* tomatoes, corn, and onion. Bring to boiling; reduce heat. Simmer, uncovered, for 10 minutes or till onion is tender, stirring occasionally.

Cut each corn muffin into *fourths*. Spoon chili over corn muffins. Sprinkle with cheese. Makes 4 servings.

Oven Directions: Prepare as directed at left, *except* put ingredients in a 1½-quart casserole instead of a skillet. Bake in a 350° oven, uncovered, for 30 minutes or till hot.

Microwave Directions: Prepare as directed at left, *except* put the ingredients in a 1½-quart microwave-safe casserole instead of a skillet. Cover and micro-cook on 100% power (high) for 6 to 8 minutes or till hot, stirring once.

Chicken Curls

EQUIPMENT
mixing bowl
dry measures
spoon
measuring spoons
12x7½x2-inch baking dish
aluminum foil
liquid measure
small saucepan
shredder
hot pads

Mild-mannered Mexican-food lovers should use mild taco sauce. For fiery-flavored curls, try hot taco sauce. No matter which spunky sauce you choose, you're sure to please every gringo in the family.

1 3-ounce package cream cheese with chives, softened ¼ cup chopped green pepper 2 tablespoons taco sauce 1 tablespoon sliced green onion 2 cups diced cooked chicken (10 ounces)	● In a mixing bowl stir together cream cheese, green pepper, taco sauce, and onion. Mix well. Stir in chicken.
8 6- or 7-inch flour tortillas	● Spoon about ¼ cup mixture along the center of each tortilla. Roll up tortillas. Place tortillas in a 12x7½x2-inch baking dish. Cover dish with foil. Bake in a 375° oven about 20 minutes. Uncover and bake for 5 minutes more.
¾ cup taco sauce ½ cup shredded mozzarella *or* cheddar cheese	● Meanwhile, in a small saucepan heat taco sauce. (*Or,* micro-cook taco sauce, uncovered, on 100% power (high) for 2 minutes, stirring once.) Spoon taco sauce over tortillas. Sprinkle with cheese. Return to oven and bake for 3 minutes more or till cheese is melted. Serves 4.

Cheesy Tater Pie

EQUIPMENT
can opener
strainer
medium mixing
  bowl
fork
dry measures
shredder
liquid measure
measuring spoons
large bowl
9-inch pie plate
hot pads

This crust takes a deliciously different twist: It's made of hash brown potatoes with bits of onion and peppers. If the potatoes are frozen together, break up them before measuring them.

1 4-ounce can mushroom stems and pieces

- Drain mushrooms.

4 eggs
1 cup diced fully cooked ham, beef, chicken, *or* turkey (5 ounces)
1 cup shredded cheddar cheese
½ cup milk
¼ teaspoon dried minced onion

- In a medium mixing bowl slightly beat eggs. Add mushrooms, meat, cheese, milk, and onion. Set aside.

2 cups frozen hash brown potatoes with onion and peppers
½ cup shredded cheddar cheese
¼ teaspoon salt
⅛ teaspoon pepper

- In a large bowl combine potatoes, cheese, salt, and pepper. Press onto bottom and up sides of an ungreased 9-inch pie plate.

- Pour egg mixture into potato crust. Bake in a 350° oven for 45 to 50 minutes or till center is set. Let pie stand for 10 minutes before serving. Makes 4 to 6 servings.

Orange-Maple Chicken

EQUIPMENT
medium skillet
measuring spoons
tongs
knife
shredder
juicer
liquid measure
small bowl
wooden spoon
serving platter
aluminum foil

As the chicken simmers, prepare the rice. When the chicken is ready, your hot, fluffy rice will be, too.

1½ pounds meaty chicken pieces (drumsticks, thighs, *or* breasts)
1 tablespoon cooking oil
1 teaspoon finely shredded orange peel
¼ cup orange juice
¼ cup water
¼ cup maple-flavored syrup
2 tablespoons prepared mustard
¼ teaspoon salt
Dash pepper

● In a medium skillet over medium-low heat slowly brown chicken pieces in hot oil about 10 minutes. In a small bowl stir together orange peel, orange juice, water, syrup, mustard, salt, and pepper.

Lightly scrape the orange down the shredder, turning it as you shred. That way you'll get only the rind, not the bitter white membrane.

● Using tongs, remove chicken from skillet. Drain fat from skillet. Return chicken to skillet. Pour orange mixture over chicken. Cover. Simmer over medium heat for 30 minutes or till chicken is done. Transfer chicken pieces to a serving platter; cover with foil.

1 tablespoon water
2 teaspoons cornstarch
Hot cooked rice

● In a small bowl stir together water and cornstarch. Add to skillet. Cook and stir till mixture is thickened and bubbly, then cook and stir for 2 minutes more. Season with salt and pepper to taste. Pour sauce over chicken. Serve with hot cooked rice. Makes 4 servings.

Cut the orange in half. Place one orange half on the juicer, as shown. While pushing down gently, twist the orange. This removes the juice from the orange.

Saucy Sausage Skillet

EQUIPMENT
knife
cutting board
measuring spoons
10-inch skillet
can opener
wooden spoon
dry measures
liquid measure
shredder

May we suggest a crisp green salad or a fresh fruit plate to go with this hearty skillet meal.

1 medium onion
1 tablespoon cooking oil
1 16-ounce can stewed tomatoes
1 cup wagon wheel macaroni *or* corkscrew macaroni
¾ cup water
1 teaspoon Italian seasoning
¼ teaspoon garlic powder
Dash bottled hot pepper sauce

● Chop onion. In a 10-inch skillet cook onion in hot oil till tender but not brown. Add *undrained* tomatoes, *uncooked* macaroni, water, Italian seasoning, garlic powder, and hot pepper sauce. Bring to boiling; reduce heat to medium-low. Cover and simmer about 20 minutes or till macaroni is tender.

2 5½-ounce packages small smoked sausage links
¾ cup shredded American, cheddar, *or* Monterey Jack cheese with jalapeño peppers

● Stir mixture. Add sausage links. Cover and cook for 5 minutes more or till heated through. Sprinkle cheese over skillet. Makes 4 servings.

EQUIPMENT

broiler pan	spoon
hot pads	dry measures
medium mixing bowl	9x9x2-inch baking pan
fork	pancake turner
measuring spoons	paper towels

Assemble your burger with one (or all) of these toppings—pickles, mustard, mayonnaise, catsup, onion, lettuce, tomato, relish, or cooked bacon. The list goes on and on.

4 hamburger buns, split

- Place hamburger buns, cut side up, on a rack in a broiler pan. Broil for 1 to 2 minutes or till golden brown. Set aside.

1 beaten egg
2 tablespoons catsup
¼ cup fine dry bread crumbs
1 tablespoon prepared mustard
¼ teaspoon onion powder
⅛ teaspoon garlic powder
Dash pepper
1 pound lean ground beef

- In a medium mixing bowl combine egg and catsup. Stir in bread crumbs, mustard, onion powder, garlic powder, and pepper. Add ground beef and mix well. Shape meat mixture into four ¾-inch-thick burgers.

4 slices cheese

- Place burgers in an ungreased 9x9x2-inch baking pan. Bake in a 425° oven for 15 to 20 minutes or till burgers are done. Using a pancake turner, transfer burgers to paper towels; drain. Place a slice of cheese on each burger. Transfer burgers to bun bottoms. Top with bun tops. Makes 4 servings.

Lemon Chicken

EQUIPMENT

paper *or* plastic bag
dry measures
measuring spoons
shredder
juicer
pastry brush
large skillet
tongs
liquid measure
spoon
hot pads
serving platter

For an international flavor, serve this tangy chicken with hot spaetzle instead of noodles. A favorite in central Europe, spaetzle (SHPETS luh) has a dumplinglike texture. You can find it in the pasta section in the grocery store.

⅓ cup all-purpose flour ½ teaspoon paprika ¼ teaspoon salt Dash pepper 1 lemon 1½ pounds meaty chicken pieces (drumsticks, thighs, *or* breasts)	● In a paper or plastic bag combine flour, paprika, salt, and pepper. Shred enough lemon peel to measure 2 teaspoons. Set aside. Squeeze juice from lemon; measure ¼ *cup* juice. Brush chicken pieces with lemon juice. Add 2 or 3 chicken pieces to bag; shake well. Repeat with remaining chicken.
2 tablespoons cooking oil ¾ cup hot water 1 teaspoon instant chicken bouillon granules ¼ cup sliced green onion 2 teaspoons sugar	● Place cooking oil in a large skillet. Heat over medium heat. Carefully place chicken pieces in oil. Cook for 5 to 10 minutes, turning once. Add hot water and bouillon granules to chicken. Stir in any remaining lemon juice, lemon peel, green onion, and sugar.
Hot cooked noodles *or* spaetzle 2 tablespoons snipped parsley (optional)	● Cover; reduce heat. Cook over low heat for 40 to 45 minutes or till chicken is tender. Place chicken pieces on a serving platter with noodles or spaetzle. Sprinkle with parsley, if you like. Skim fat from sauce; pass with chicken. Makes 4 servings.

Spanish-Style Pork Chops

EQUIPMENT
knife
10-inch skillet
pancake turner
liquid measure
cutting board
can opener
kitchen scissors
spoon

4 pork chops, cut ½ inch thick (about 1½ pounds)
1 tablespoon margarine *or* butter
½ cup water

• Trim excess fat from chops. Melt margarine or butter in a 10-inch skillet. Brown chops in hot margarine for 5 minutes. Add water. Cover and simmer for 20 minutes.

½ of a small green pepper
½ of a small onion
1 16-ounce can tomatoes
1 4½-ounce package regular Spanish-style rice mix
¼ cup water

• Chop green pepper and onion. Using kitchen scissors, cut up tomatoes in can. Add green pepper, onion, *undrained* tomatoes, *uncooked* rice mix, and water. Spoon liquid over rice. Cover and simmer for 20 minutes more or till chops are done and rice is tender. Let stand for 10 minutes before serving. Serves 4.

Oven Method: Trim and brown chops as directed at left. Snip tomatoes in can. In a 2-quart casserole combine *undrained* tomatoes, *uncooked* rice mix, water, chopped green pepper, and chopped onion. Place browned chops on top of rice mixture. Cover and bake in a 350° oven for 1 hour or till pork chops and rice are tender. Let stand for 10 minutes before serving.

Baked Ham With Plum Sauce

EQUIPMENT
small saucepan
measuring spoons
wooden spoon
shallow baking pan
hot pads
pancake turners
serving plate

1 12-ounce jar plum preserves (1 cup)
1 tablespoon brown sugar
1 tablespoon vinegar
1 teaspoon dried minced onion
¼ teaspoon dried minced garlic
¼ teaspoon crushed red pepper
¼ teaspoon ground ginger

• For sauce, in a small saucepan stir together plum preserves, brown sugar, vinegar, onion, garlic, red pepper, and ginger. Bring mixture to boiling, stirring constantly. Remove from the heat.

1 pound fully cooked ham slice, cut ½ inch thick

• Place ham in a shallow baking pan. Pour *half* of the sauce over ham. Bake, uncovered, in a 350° oven for 15 minutes. Transfer ham to a serving plate. Reheat remaining sauce. Serve with ham. Makes 5 servings.

This delicate plum sauce was a hit with our teen testers—and some thought it would be good on chicken, too. If you'd like to try it on chicken, prepare sauce as directed at left. Place 4 boneless, skinless *chicken breast halves* (about 1 pound) in an 8x8x2-inch baking dish. Pour *half* of the sauce over chicken. Bake, covered, in a 350° oven for 30 to 35 minutes or till chicken is tender. Reheat remaining sauce. Serve with chicken. Makes 4 servings.

Tuna Turnovers

EQUIPMENT

can opener	measuring spoons
strainer	wooden spoon
knife	fork
cutting board	baking sheet
vegetable peeler	small bowl
shredder	pastry brush
mixing bowl	hot pads

1 9¼-ounce can tuna 2 stalks celery ½ of a medium green pepper 2 medium carrots 1 8-ounce container soft-style cream cheese with chives and onion ¼ teaspoon pepper	● Drain tuna; set aside. Chop celery and green pepper. Shred carrots. In a mixing bowl stir together cream cheese, celery, green pepper, carrot, and pepper. Using a fork, flake tuna into bowl. Stir into cream cheese mixture.
2 9-inch folded refrigerated unbaked piecrusts	● Unfold piecrusts; cut each in half. Spoon *one-fourth* of the filling onto *half* of one piece of pie crust. Moisten pastry edges with water. Gently lift and fold other half of piecrust over filling. Seal edges with the tines of a fork (see photo, right). Repeat with remaining piecrust pieces and filling. Place turnovers on a baking sheet.
1 beaten egg	● Brush turnovers with egg. Cut slits in dough to let steam escape. Bake in a 375° oven about 25 minutes or till golden brown. Let stand for 10 to 15 minutes on baking sheet before serving. Makes 4 servings.

If you want to serve only one or two now, wrap remaining *unbaked* turnovers in foil. Seal, label, and freeze.

To reheat, place frozen turnover(s) on a greased baking sheet. Brush with egg. Cut slits in dough. Bake in a 400° oven about 30 minutes or till golden brown. Let stand for 10 to 15 minutes before serving.

Moisten edges of pastry with a little water. Fold pastry over filling. Gently seal edges of turnovers with the tines of a fork. This keeps the filling from seeping out.

Favorite Fried Chicken

We've made old-fashioned fried chicken extra-easy by cooking it in the oven. While the chicken is baking, make the Couscous Salad. Then catch up on homework, practice the piano, or shoot some hoops. During the last 15 minutes the chicken is in the oven, pull the rest of the meal together for a fast-paced finish. (See recipes, page 62.)

MENU

Dilled Fried Chicken
Couscous Salad
Breadsticks or rolls
Fresh fruit
Milk

MENU COUNTDOWN

1 Hour Ahead:
Prepare Dilled Fried Chicken. Place in oven.
Start Couscous Salad. Cover and chill.

15 Minutes Ahead:
Clean fresh fruit. Cut into pieces, if you like.
Pour milk into glasses.
Place breadsticks or rolls in a basket.

Dilled Fried Chicken

Pictured on pages 60 and 61.

Fried chicken makes a delicious outdoor meal after a busy day of bookwork.

	EQUIPMENT	
	dry measures	knife
	plastic bag	measuring spoons
	rolling pin	spoon
	waxed paper *or* pie plate	pastry brush
		shallow baking pan
	small saucepan	hot pads

1½ cups bite-size wheat, rice, *or* corn square cereal	● Place cereal in a plastic bag. Close tightly. Using a rolling pin, crush cereal. Transfer to waxed paper or a pie plate.
3 tablespoons margarine *or* butter 1 teaspoon dried dillweed 2 pounds meaty chicken pieces (drumsticks, thighs, *or* breasts)	● In a small saucepan stir together margarine or butter, dillweed, ¼ teaspoons *salt*, and ⅛ teaspoon *pepper*. Heat and stir till margarine is melted. Brush chicken pieces with margarine mixture. Roll chicken in cereal to coat.
	● Place chicken, skin side up, in an ungreased shallow baking pan so pieces aren't touching one another. Bake in a 375° oven about 50 minutes or till tender. Makes 4 servings.

Couscous Salad

Pictured on pages 60 and 61.

Couscous (KOO skoos) is tiny, pastalike pieces formed from ground wheat and water. Even though it's a North African ingredient, it tastes just like American pasta. Look for it next to other pasta in the grocery store.

	EQUIPMENT	
	knife	dry measures
	cutting board	measuring spoons
	shredder	spoon
	medium bowl	screw-top jar

1 small tomato 1 small carrot ½ of a small zucchini *or* cucumber ¼ cup ready-to-cook couscous 1 tablespoon sliced green onion 1 tablespoon sliced black olives	● Core and chop tomato. Shred carrot. Cut zucchini or cucumber into thin strips, about the size of a matchstick. In a medium bowl combine tomato, carrot, zucchini or cucumber, *uncooked* couscous, green onion, and olives.
1 tablespoon salad oil 1 tablespoon vinegar 1 teaspoon sugar ⅛ teaspoon dried basil ¼ teaspoon Dijon-style mustard	● In a screw-top jar combine salad oil, vinegar, 1 tablespoon *water,* sugar, basil, mustard, dash *salt* and dash *pepper*. Cover and shake well. Pour over couscous mixture; toss to coat. Cover and chill. Makes 4 servings.

Country Casserole

EQUIPMENT
knife
cutting board
large saucepan
wooden spoon
measuring spoons
liquid measure
dry measures
1-quart casserole
kitchen scissors
hot pads

You're going to love last night's leftovers! By substituting leftover chicken, turkey, or beef for the ham, and adding ¼ teaspoon salt, you can create a new family favorite.

1 small stalk celery ½ of a medium onion ½ of a small green pepper 2 tablespoons margarine *or* butter	● Chop celery, onion, and green pepper. In a large saucepan cook celery, onion, and green pepper in margarine or butter till vegetables are tender.
3 tablespoons all-purpose flour ¼ teaspoon dried basil Dash pepper 1⅓ cups milk	● Stir in flour, basil, and pepper. Stir in milk all at once. Cook and stir till thickened and bubbly, then cook and stir for 1 minute more.
1½ cups cubed fully cooked ham (about 8 ounces) ⅔ cup cooked green beans, carrots, peas, corn, *or* mixed vegetables 1 package (6) refrigerated biscuits	● Stir ham and vegetables into mixture. Pour into a 1-quart casserole. Using kitchen scissors, snip biscuits into quarters (see photo, below). Place on top of mixture. Bake in a 400° oven about 15 minutes or till mixture is heated through and biscuits are lightly browned. Let stand for 5 minutes. Makes 4 servings.

Using kitchen scissors, snip each biscuit into quarters.

1 Stir the ingredients together in a small bowl.

2 Spread 2 tablespoons of filling in the center of each chicken breast.

Chicken Bundles

EQUIPMENT
small mixing bowl
strainer
shredder
dry meaures
measuring spoons
spoon
knife
wooden toothpicks
10x6x2-inch baking dish
small saucepan
pastry brush
hot pads

- 1 2½-ounce jar sliced mushrooms, drained
- ¼ cup shredded mozzarella or Monterey Jack cheese (1 ounce)
- ¼ cup plain yogurt
- 1 tablespoon chopped pimiento
- 2 teaspoons dried parsley flakes
- 4 boned skinless chicken breast halves (about 1 pound)

● In a mixing bowl stir together drained mushrooms, cheese, yogurt, pimiento, and parsley flakes. Spread *2 rounded tablespoons* of mixture on each piece of chicken. Fold 1 side over to meet other. Fasten with wooden toothpicks.

- 1 tablespoon margarine or butter
- Grated Parmesan cheese

● Place chicken bundles, toothpick side up, in a 10x6x2-inch baking dish. In a small saucepan melt margarine or butter. Brush tops with melted margarine. Sprinkle with Parmesan cheese. Bake in a 350° oven for 40 to 45 minutes. Makes 4 servings.

65 Ready, Set, Start Supper

3 After brushing the tops of the chicken breasts with margarine, sprinkle with Parmesan cheese.

Turkey and Trimmings

EQUIPMENT
small saucepan
knife
2 mixing bowls
liquid measure
wooden spoon
can opener
dry measures
measuring spoons
10-ounce custard cups
shallow baking pan or baking sheet
hot pads

Enjoy a Thanksgiving feast any night of the week. This dinnertime dish has all your holiday favorites in one dish—turkey, gravy, stuffing, and cranberry sauce.

---

3 tablespoons margarine *or* butter
1 8-ounce package corn bread stuffing mix
⅔ cup hot water
1 10½-ounce can *or* one 12-ounce jar turkey gravy
1½ cups cubed cooked turkey *or* chicken (about 8 ounces)
¼ teaspoon onion powder

● In a small saucepan melt margarine or butter. In a mixing bowl combine stuffing mix, hot water, and margarine.
   In another bowl combine gravy, turkey or chicken, and onion powder.

¼ cup chopped pecans
1 tablespoon snipped parsley (optional)

● Pat *one-fourth* of the stuffing mixture onto the bottom and up the sides of a 10-ounce custard cup. Repeat with 3 more cups.
   Spoon *one-fourth* of the gravy mixture into each cup. Sprinkle with chopped pecans. Sprinkle with parsley, if you like.

Cranberry sauce (optional)

● Place custard cups in a shallow baking pan or on a baking sheet. Bake in a 350° oven for 40 minutes. Serve with cranberry sauce, if you like. Serves 4.

Pork Loaf With Cranberry Sauce

EQUIPMENT

plastic bag	small mixing bowl
rolling pin	spoon
medium mixing bowl	dry measures
fork	hot pads
measuring spoons	2 pancake turners
11x7x2-inch baking pan	serving platter

When you make meat loaf, meatballs, or burgers, the best way to mix everything is with your hands. Keep your hands clean by wearing plastic gloves or plastic bags on them.

---

8 whole wheat crackers
1 egg
2 tablespoons dried minced onion
1 tablespoon dried parsley flakes
¼ teaspoon salt
¼ teaspoon prepared mustard
⅛ teaspoon ground sage
Dash pepper

● Place whole wheat crackers in a plastic bag. Close tightly. Using a rolling pin, crush crackers.
In a medium mixing bowl beat egg. Stir in crackers, onion, parsley, salt, mustard, sage, and pepper.

---

1 pound lean ground pork

● Add pork. Using hands, mix well. In a 11x7x2-inch baking pan, pat mixture into a loaf about 6 inches long and 3 inches wide. Bake, uncovered, in a 350° oven for 50 minutes, or till no longer pink.

¼ cup cranberry-orange sauce
2 tablespoons catsup

● In a small mixing bowl stir together cranberry-orange sauce and catsup; spoon atop loaf. Bake for 3 to 4 minutes more to heat through. Use 2 pancake turners to transfer pork loaf to a serving platter. Makes 4 servings.

California Pizza

Peanutty Stuffed Pears

Mamma Mia, It's A Pizza!

Make dinnertime party time with this fast food delight. American cheese, Tex-Mex, Italian, California, or German toppers give your pizza an around-the-world flavor. Set out your family's favorite toppings and then let each partygoer top his or her own pizza. (See recipes, pages 70 and 71.)

MENU

By-the-Slice Pizza
Garden Salad
Peanutty Stuffed Pears
Lemonade

MENU COUNTDOWN

30 Minutes Ahead:
Prepare Peanutty Stuffed Pears. Cover and chill.

20 Minutes Ahead:
Place crescent rolls for By-the-Slice Pizza on a baking sheet and prebake. Assemble pizza ingredients. Make Garden Salad.

10 Minutes Ahead:
Top pizza slices and bake. Pour lemonade into glasses.

Garden Salad

By-the-Slice Pizza

Pictured on pages 68 and 69.

Pizza's a personal thing. This recipe lets you create made-to-order flavors for your whole family. Do all the cooking yourself. Or, take it easy and let all the family members top their own pizzas.

EQUIPMENT
baking sheet
hot pads
dry measures
can opener
spoons
shredder

1 8-ounce package (8) refrigerated crescent rolls	● Unroll crescent rolls. Divide along *short* perforations to form 4 rectangles. Pat the diagonal perforations together to seal seam. Place rectangles on a baking sheet. Bake in a 375° oven for 10 minutes.
¼ cup grated Parmesan cheese 1 8-ounce can pizza sauce Tex-Mex, German, California, *or* Italian Topping 1 cup shredded cheese	● Sprinkle Parmesan cheese over rolls. Top with pizza sauce. Top with desired topping. Sprinkle pizzas with shredded cheese. Bake for 6 to 7 minutes or till heated through. Makes 4 servings.

Tex-Mex Topping: Arrange drained, diced *green chili peppers* atop slices. Sprinkle with cheese and continue as directed. Top with *dairy sour cream* and crushed *tortilla chips.* Serve with *taco sauce,* if you like.

German Topping: Arrange drained and snipped *sauerkraut* and diced *fully cooked ham* atop slices. Sprinkle with cheese and continue as directed.

California Topping: Arrange chopped *avocado* and diced cooked *chicken* atop slices. Sprinkle with cheese and continue as directed. Top with *alfalfa sprouts.*

Italian Topping: Arrange sliced *mushrooms* and sliced fully cooked *sausage or pepperoni* atop slices. Sprinkle with cheese and sliced *black olives.* Continue as directed.

Garden Salad

Pictured on page 69.

EQUIPMENT
shredder
large bowl
knife
cutting board
measuring spoons
dry measures

Top with your favorite dressing—and any other ingredients you'd like to help spruce up your salad.

1 medium carrot
2 cups torn lettuce
½ of a small cucumber, thinly sliced
¼ cup walnuts
2 or 3 tablespoons Italian salad dressing
Sliced radishes (optional)

● Shred carrot. In a large bowl combine carrot, lettuce, cucumber, and walnuts. Pour dressing over mixture. Toss to coat. Add radishes, if you like. Serves 4.

Peanutty Stuffed Pears

Pictured on page 69.

EQUIPMENT
small bowl
measuring spoons
spoon
knife
cutting board
melon baller
pastry brush

Wow! Here's a dessert that has it all: terrific taste, subtle sweetness, and easy instructions.

3 tablespoons soft-style cream cheese
3 tablespoons chunky peanut butter
1 tablespoon orange juice
1 teaspoon honey
3 tablespoons chopped mixed dried fruit
1 tablespoon sunflower nuts

● In a small bowl stir together cream cheese and peanut butter. Add orange juice, stirring till well mixed.
Stir in honey. Stir in dried fruit and sunflower nuts.

2 medium pears
1 teaspoon lemon juice
1 teaspoon water

● Cut pears in half lengthwise. With a melon baller, hollow out core and discard. Hollow out pear to within ½ inch of edge. Reserve pear pulp.
Combine lemon juice and water; brush over cut surfaces of pear.

Sunflower nuts (optional)

● Chop pear pulp; stir into peanut butter mixture. Fill pears with mixture. Sprinkle with additional sunflower nuts, if you like. Makes 4 servings.

72 All for One and One for All

CAUTION DASHING DINERS

When busy schedules transform dinnertime into disaster time, lend Mom and Dad a hand in the kitchen. The recipes in this chapter will let you prepare dinner in shifts. Make each recipe now and serve it to those who are ready to eat. Then, for those on the go, *Dashing Diners* gives reheating directions so everyone can enjoy your home cooking, no matter how long activities last.

Tempting Tuna Salad

EQUIPMENT
small bowls
dry measures
measuring spoons
spoon
knife
cutting board
can opener
strainer
fork
large bowl
serving plates

Brrrr! Like your salad icy cold? Before you leave for school in the morning (or the night before), place the cans of tuna, pineapple, and oranges in the refrigerator.

¼ cup mayonnaise *or* salad dressing
¼ cup plain yogurt
½ teaspoon curry powder (optional)
1 apple
1 8-ounce can pineapple tidbits (juice pack)

● For dressing, in a small bowl combine mayonnaise or salad dressing and yogurt. Stir in curry powder, if you like.
  Core and chop apple. Drain pineapple, reserving liquid. Toss apple in pineapple liquid. Drain.

1 stalk celery
1 12½-ounce can tuna
1 11-ounce can mandarin orange sections *or* 1 cup seedless grapes
 Lettuce leaves *or* chow mein noodles
¼ cup chopped peanuts

● Chop celery. Drain tuna. Drain orange sections. Using a fork, flake tuna into a large bowl. Add pineapple, apple, celery, orange sections or grapes, and dressing. Set aside desired portions. (See *Dashing Diners.*) Toss to mix. Arrange lettuce or chow mein noodles on individual serving plates. Spoon salad atop. Sprinkle with peanuts. Makes 4 servings.

Dashing Diners: Cover and chill set-aside portions of salad and dressing separately. Before serving, toss and assemble as directed above.

Egg-Salad Roll Ups

EQUIPMENT
knife
cutting board
medium mixing
  bowl
shredder
dry measures
measuring spoons
wooden spoon
liquid measure
spoon

6 hard-cooked eggs
½ cup shredded cheese
2 tablespoons sweet pickle relish
1 tablespoon finely chopped green onion
1 teaspoon dried parsley flakes
⅓ cup bacon and tomato salad dressing *or* creamy cucumber salad dressing

● Peel and chop eggs. In a medium mixing bowl combine eggs, cheese, pickle relish, onion, and parsley. Pour dressing over mixture. Toss to coat.

Shredded lettuce *or* **leaf lettuce**
4 8-inch flour tortillas

● To serve, place some lettuce on each tortilla. Set aside desired portions. (See *Dashing Diners.*) Spoon about *½ cup* filling down center of each tortilla. Roll up. Makes 4 servings.

Dashing Diners: Do not assemble Roll Ups. Cover and chill set-aside portions of egg mixture. Before serving, assemble as directed above.

Looking for clues leading to perfectly cooked eggs? Here are the hard facts:
● Place eggs in shells in a large saucepan.
● Add enough cold water to cover eggs. Bring to a rapid boil over high heat.
● Reduce the heat so the water is just below simmering; cover.
● Cook for 15 to 20 minutes. Pour off water.
● Add cold water; let stand for at least 2 minutes.

Super Spuds

EQUIPMENT
vegetable brush
fork
aluminum foil
hot pads
knife

4 large baking potatoes (7 to 8 ounces each)
Texas Taters, German Spuds, Italian Taters, *or* Potatoes O'Connor

● Scrub baking potatoes with a brush. Prick potatoes with a fork. Wrap in squares of foil. Bake in a 425° oven for 40 to 60 minutes. Meanwhile, prepare desired topper. Set aside desired number of portions. (See *Dashing Diners.*) Unwrap potatoes. Using hot pads, roll gently under your hands. Cut a crisscross in the top. Press ends; push up. Spoon topper over potatoes. Makes 4 servings.

Dashing Diners: Cover and chill set-aside topper. Leave potatoes in foil. Place in turned-off oven. Before serving, place topper in a saucepan. Cook and stir over medium heat till heated through. Spoon over potatoes.

Texas Taters: In a saucepan heat one 15½-ounce can *chili with beans* and 1 cup shredded *cheddar cheese.* Divide mixture among 4 baked potatoes.
 Sprinkle potatoes with ½ cup shredded *cheddar cheese* and sliced *green onion,* if you like.

German Spuds: In a saucepan heat one 8-ounce can *undrained sauerkraut* and 12 ounces *smoked sausage links,* cut into bite-size pieces. Drain.
 Stir in 1 tablespoon *Thousand Island salad dressing.* Divide mixture among 4 baked potatoes. Sprinkle with ½ cup shredded *caraway cheese.* Pass additional dressing, if you like.

Italian Taters: In a saucepan heat one 15½-ounce jar *spaghetti sauce with meat,* and one 3½- or 4-ounce package *sliced pepperoni,* halved. Divide mixture among 4 baked potatoes. Sprinkle with ½ cup shredded *mozzarella cheese.* (Or, substitute 4 ounces chopped *fully cooked ham, chicken, or turkey* for pepperoni.)

Potatoes O' Connor: In a saucepan melt 1 tablespoon *margarine or butter.* Add ¼ cup chopped *onion,* ¼ teaspoon *garlic salt,* and ⅛ teaspoon *pepper.* Cook and stir till onion is tender but not brown. Stir in 2 tablespoons all-purpose *flour.* Add 1¾ cups *milk.* Cook and stir till thickened and bubbly.
 Add one 3-ounce package *cream cheese,* cut up. Heat and stir till melted. Stir in two 3-ounce packages *very thinly sliced corned beef,* cut up; 2 teaspoons dried *parsley flakes;* and ½ cup finely chopped *cabbage.* Heat through. Divide mixture among 4 baked potatoes.

Easy Potato-Sausage Chowder

EQUIPMENT
medium saucepan
dry measures
liquid measure
measuring spoons
can opener
wooden spoon
knife

Draw, pardner! If you need a quick draw at dinnertime, this soup is your answer. In less than 20 minutes you can have a hearty helping of this cheesy chowder chasing the hungries away.

- 2 cups frozen loose-pack hash brown potatoes
- 1 cup loose-pack frozen mixed cauliflower, broccoli, and carrots
- ½ cup water
- 1 tablespoon dried minced onion

● In a medium saucepan combine potatoes, vegetables, water, and onion. Bring to boiling; reduce heat. Cover and simmer about 3 minutes.

- 1 11-ounce can condensed cheddar cheese soup
- 1½ cups milk
- ⅛ teaspoon pepper

● Stir in soup; mix well. Stir in milk and pepper. Cook over medium heat till bubbly. Simmer, covered, for 5 minutes.

- 8 ounces fully cooked smoked turkey sausage *or* hot dogs, cut into ½-inch pieces

● Add sausage or hot dogs. Cook for 5 minutes more or till heated through. Set aside desired portions. (See *Dashing Diners*.) Makes 4 servings.

Microwave Directions: In a 2-quart casserole combine potatoes, vegetables, water, and onion. Micro-cook, covered, on 100% power (high) for 4 to 5 minutes. Stir in soup, milk, and pepper. Micro-cook, covered, on high for 5 minutes more. Add sausage. Micro-cook, covered, on high for 3 minutes more or till heated through.

Dashing Diners: Cool set-aside portions of soup. Cover and chill. Before serving, place soup in a saucepan. Cook over medium heat about 6 minutes or till mixture is heated through.

Orange-Poached Fish

EQUIPMENT
large skillet
liquid measure
measuring spoons
vegetable peeler
cutting board
knife
wooden spoon
fork
pancake turner
serving platter
aluminum foil
small bowl

If you like, serve this dish with hot cooked rice or hot noodles so you can enjoy every drop of the scrumptious orange sauce.

1 cup orange juice 2 tablespoons soy sauce 2 stalks celery, thinly sliced 2 medium carrots, thinly sliced	● In a large skillet combine orange juice and soy sauce. Add celery and carrots. Bring mixture to boiling; reduce heat. Cover and simmer for 6 to 8 minutes or till vegetables are crisp-tender. Push vegetables to side of skillet.
1 11-ounce package frozen fish portions	● Place frozen fish portions in a single layer in center of skillet. Bring to boiling; reduce heat. Cover and simmer about 9 minutes or till fish flakes easily with a fork. Using a pancake turner, transfer fish to a serving platter. Cover with foil.
¼ cup cold water 1 tablespoon cornstarch	● In a small bowl stir together water and cornstarch. Add to orange juice in skillet. Cook and stir till thickened and bubbly, then cook and stir for 2 minutes more. Set aside desired portions. (See *Dashing Diners*.) Pour mixture over fish. Serves 4.
	Dashing Diners: Place set-aside portions in foil. Chill. Reheat in a 400° oven for 15 minutes. (*Or,* do not wrap in foil. Place reserved portions in a casserole; cover. Micro-cook on 100% power (high) about 1½ minutes or till heated through.)

Whole-in-One Pizza

EQUIPMENT
8-inch skillet
wooden spoon
strainer
large bowl
can opener
measuring spoons
2-inch round cutter
baking sheet
hot pads

Fore! Watch out for the great taste of these sandwiches. One taste and you'll know you're right on par with these pizzawiches.

8 ounces ground beef, turkey, *or* pork 1 8-ounce can pizza sauce 1 teaspoon dried minced onion	● In an 8-inch skillet cook ground meat till brown. Drain off fat (see photo, right). Stir in pizza sauce and onion. Cover and simmer for 5 minutes or till mixture is heated through.
4 hamburger buns, split	● Meanwhile, use a 2-inch round cutter to cut a hole in the *top* of each bun. Reserve bun centers for another use. Place buns cut side up on a baking sheet. Broil 4 inches from heat about 2 minutes or till golden brown. Set aside desired number of portions. (See *Dashing Diners*.)
2 slices mozzarella cheese, halved	● Place a cheese slice on each bun bottom. (If you like, broil buns for 30 seconds more or till cheese is melted.) Place tops on buns. Evenly divide hot pizza mixture among buns. Serves 4.

Dashing Diners: Do not place cheese on bun or fill with mixture. Cover and chill set-aside portions of meat. Before serving, place meat mixture in a saucepan. Cook and stir over medium heat till mixture is heated through. Assemble as directed above.

To drain the cooked ground meat, place a strainer over a large bowl. Carefully spoon the meat into the strainer, as shown. Let stand for several minutes to allow the fat to drain completely.

Creamy Ham And Veggies

A delicious way to enjoy veggies, even if you're not a vegetable fan.

EQUIPMENT
medium saucepan liquid measure
knife dry measures
wooden spoon toaster
measuring spoons plates

- 3 tablespoons margarine *or* butter
- 1 10-ounce package frozen mixed vegetables
- 3 tablespoons all-purpose flour
- ¼ teaspoon salt
- Dash pepper
- 1½ cups milk

● In a saucepan melt margarine or butter over high heat. Add vegetables. Cover and simmer over medium-low heat for 4 to 5 minutes or till tender, stirring once. Stir in flour, salt, and pepper. Add milk all at once. Cook and stir over medium heat till mixture is thickened and bubbly.

- 1½ cups cubed fully cooked ham (about 8 ounces)
- 1 tablespoon prepared mustard

● Stir in ham and mustard. Cook for 1 minute more or till heated through. Set aside desired number of portions. (See *Dashing Diners*.)

- 4 English muffins, split, *or* 4 slices bread

● Meanwhile, toast English muffins or bread. Place *2* muffin halves or *1* bread slice on an individual plate. Spoon ham mixture atop. Repeat with remaining muffins. Makes 4 servings.

Dashing Diners: Do not toast English muffins or bread. Cover and chill set-aside ham mixture. Before serving, toast English muffins or bread. Place ham mixture in a saucepan. Cook and stir over medium heat till heated through. Assemble as directed above.

Orange-Chicken Delight

EQUIPMENT
baking pan
hot pads
large saucepans
colander
liquid measure
dry measures
measuring spoons
wooden spoon
2-quart casserole

Fines herbes is a blend of parsley, tarragon, basil, thyme, and chives.

½ cup sliced almonds

- Place almonds in a shallow baking pan. Bake in a 350° oven for 5 to 10 minutes. (*Or,* place almonds in a 9-inch microwave-safe pie plate. Micro-cook on 100% power (high) for 5 to 6 minutes.)

4 cups wide egg noodles

- In a large saucepan cook noodles in a large amount of boiling lightly salted water for 10 to 12 minutes or till tender. Drain; set aside.

1½ cups chicken broth
½ cup frozen orange juice concentrate, thawed
2 tablespoons cornstarch
½ teaspoon fines herbes
2 cups diced cooked chicken (10 ounces)

- Meanwhile, in a large saucepan stir together chicken broth, orange juice concentrate, cornstarch, and fines herbes. Cook and stir till thickened and bubbly, then cook and stir for 2 minutes more. Stir in cooked noodles and chicken.

- Turn mixture into a 2-quart casserole. Bake, uncovered, in a 350° oven for 15 to 20 minutes or till heated through. Sprinkle with almonds. Set aside desired portions. (See *Dashing Diners.*) Serves 6.

Dashing Diners: Cover and chill set-aside portions of chicken mixture. Before serving, place mixture in a saucepan. Cook mixture over medium heat till heated through.

Cranberries And Turkey

EQUIPMENT
medium saucepan   dry measures
spoon   measuring spoons

So simple and so sensational! It's the cranberry sauce that adds a tang to this four-ingredient suppertime success.

1 10-ounce package frozen rice and wild rice with green beans and mushrooms	● In a medium saucepan cook rice according to package directions.
2 cups cubed smoked fully cooked turkey breast (about 10 ounces) 2 tablespoons water ¼ cup whole-berry cranberry sauce	● Stir in turkey and water. Heat mixture through, stirring occasionally. Stir in cranberry sauce; heat for 1 minute more. Set aside desired portions. (See *Dashing Diners*.) Makes 4 servings.

Microwave Directions: Omit water. In a 2-quart casserole cook frozen rice and vegetable mixture in the microwave oven according to package directions. Stir in smoked turkey.

Micro-cook, uncovered, on 100% power (high) for 2 to 3 minutes or till the mixture is heated through, stirring once. Stir in cranberry sauce. Micro-cook on high for 30 seconds more.

Dashing Diners: Cover and chill set-aside mixture. Before serving, return mixture to saucepan. Cook mixture over medium heat till heated through.

Sausage Soup

EQUIPMENT

large saucepan	cutting board
can opener	dry measures
measuring spoons	wooden spoon
knife	shredder

- 2 14½-ounce cans beef broth
- ½ teaspoon caraway seed
- ¼ teaspoon pepper
- ⅛ teaspoon garlic powder
- ¾ pound fully cooked Polish sausage, cut into ½-inch slices
- 2 cups frozen hash brown potatoes with onion and peppers

● In a large saucepan combine beef broth, caraway seed, pepper, and garlic powder. Bring to boiling; reduce heat. Add sausage, and frozen potatoes. Cook, covered, for 5 minutes.

- 2 cups coarsely shredded cabbage
- 1 9-ounce package frozen peas and carrots
- 1 large apple, cored and chopped (optional)

● Stir in cabbage and peas and carrots. Stir in apple, if you like. Cook about 5 minutes or till cabbage is crisp-tender. Set aside desired portions. (See *Dashing Diners.*) Makes 4 servings.

Dashing Diners: Cover and chill set-aside portions of soup. Before serving, return soup to saucepan. Cook and stir over medium heat till heated through.

Serve these breadsticks with Sausage Soup to make a warming wintertime menu.

Cheese Fingers: Stir together 2 tablespoons softened *margarine or butter* and ¼ teaspoon *garlic powder*. Place 4 *bread slices* on a baking sheet. Broil 4 inches from the heat about 1 minute or till lightly browned. Remove from the oven. Cool slightly. Turn over bread slices. Spread with margarine mixture. Sprinkle with ¼ cup grated *Parmesan cheese.* Broil for 1 to 2 minutes more or till lightly browned. Cut each slice into 4 sticks. Makes 4 servings.

Chicken Tacos

EQUIPMENT
aluminum foil	wooden spoon
small saucepan	knife
dry measures	cutting board
can opener	hot pads
measuring spoons	spoon

6 taco shells	● Wrap taco shells in foil. Warm in a 300° oven for 8 to 10 minutes.
2 cups diced cooked chicken *or* turkey (10 ounces) 1 8-ounce can tomato sauce ½ teaspoon dried oregano ⅛ teaspoon garlic powder	● Meanwhile, in a small saucepan stir together chicken, tomato sauce, oregano, and garlic powder. Cook and stir over medium heat for 5 minutes.
1 medium tomato 1 cup shredded lettuce 1 cup shredded American *or* cheddar cheese Taco sauce (optional)	● Core and chop tomato. Remove taco shells from foil. Spoon about ¼ cup chicken mixture into each shell. Set aside desired portions. (See *Dashing Diners*.) Top with lettuce, tomato, and cheese. Top with taco sauce, if you like. Makes 3 servings.

Dashing Diners: Do not assemble tacos. Cover and chill set-aside chicken mixture. Keep taco shells in foil in a warm oven. Before serving, place chicken mixture in a small saucepan. Cook over medium heat till heated through. Assemble as directed.

Although most Americans consider tacos hard tortilla shells filled with a spicy beef mixture, they are truly much more. Tacos are considered the Mexican sandwich. They can be stuffed with a variety of fillings and are eaten warmed, grilled, fried, or baked.

Spaghetti and Meatballs

EQUIPMENT
bowl
liquid measure
dry measures
fork
knife
cutting board
measuring spoons
shallow baking pan
hot pads
medium saucepan
can opener
wooden spoon
Dutch oven
strainer

Need to keep pasta hot for a short time? Just remember this little rhyme:
  Place drained pasta in the cooking pot.
  Add margarine, then cover, to keep it hot.

1 egg
¼ cup milk
1 cup soft bread crumbs
¼ cup finely chopped onion
¼ teaspoon salt
12 ounces ground beef *or* ground pork

● In a bowl combine egg and milk; stir in bread crumbs, onion, and salt. Add ground beef or pork. Using hands, mix well. Shape into sixteen 1-inch balls.

● Place meatballs in a shallow baking pan. Bake in a 400° oven for 15 minutes or till meatballs are done.

1 10¾-ounce can condensed tomato soup
1 6-ounce can tomato paste
⅔ cup (5½-ounce can) apple juice
¼ cup water
1 teaspoon Italian seasoning

● Meanwhile, in a medium saucepan stir together tomato soup, tomato paste, apple juice, water, and Italian seasoning. Cover and simmer for 15 minutes, stirring occasionally.

● Add meatballs to sauce. Cover; simmer for 10 minutes more.

8 ounces spaghetti

● While meatballs are cooking, bring a large amount of water to boil in a Dutch oven or large saucepan. Add spaghetti. Cook for 10 to 12 minutes or till spaghetti is tender but slightly firm. Stir occasionally. Drain spaghetti.

Grated Parmesan cheese

● Set aside desired number of portions. (See *Dashing Diners.*) Serve sauce and meatballs atop hot spaghetti. Top with Parmesan cheese. Makes 4 servings.

Dashing Diners: Combine set-aside portions of sauce and spaghetti in an ovenproof dish. Cover. Keep warm in a 200° oven. Stir before serving. Serve with Parmesan cheese.

Saucy Chicken Cups

EQUIPMENT
10-ounce custard cups
pastry brush
baking sheet
medium saucepan
strainer
can opener
dry measures
measuring spoons
wooden spoon
hot pads

Let's face it: Favorite veggies vary from cook to cook. Make this recipe to suit your taste by substituting corn, green beans, peas, broccoli, carrots, or any other frozen vegetable(s) you like for the ones we've suggested.

3 6-inch flour tortillas	● Grease three 10-ounce custard cups. Brush each tortilla with a little water. Fit each tortilla into a prepared custard cup. Place custard cups on a baking sheet. Bake in a 350° oven for 12 to 15 minutes or just till light brown.
2 cups loose-pack frozen mixed broccoli, corn, and red peppers 1 cup diced cooked chicken (5 ounces) 1 7¼-ounce can semi-condensed cream of tomato *or* mushroom soup 1 teaspoon Worcestershire sauce	● Meanwhile, prepare frozen vegetables according to package directions. Drain. Return vegetables to saucepan. Stir in chicken, soup, and Worcestershire sauce. Cook, stirring occasionally, over medium heat about 5 minutes or till mixture is heated through. Set aside desired portions. (See *Dashing Diners*.) Spoon into tortilla cups. Makes 3 servings.
	Dashing Diners: Cover and chill set-aside portions of vegetable mixture. Before serving, place vegetable mixture in a saucepan. Cook and stir over medium heat till heated through. Spoon into tortilla cups.

First, brush each tortilla lightly with water. This keeps it moist and prevents it from cracking. Place the tortilla over a prepared custard cup. Using your fingers, gently press down in the middle of the tortilla and shape it into a ruffle, as shown.

By-the-Sea Chowder

EQUIPMENT
- knife
- 2-quart saucepan
- wooden spoon
- measuring spoons
- liquid measure
- can opener
- strainer
- fork

Ahoy landlubber. If you're not a tuna lover, try making this cheesy soup with chicken. Just substitute 1½ cups cubed cooked chicken for the tuna—it's that easy.

2 tablespoons margarine *or* butter 1 10-ounce package frozen mixed vegetables	● In a 2-quart saucepan melt margarine or butter. Add vegetables. Cook, covered, over medium heat about 10 minutes or till vegetables are tender.
2 tablespoons all-purpose flour ½ teaspoon dried basil ¼ teaspoon salt ⅛ teaspoon pepper 2½ cups milk	● Stir in flour, basil, salt, and pepper. Add milk. Cook and stir till slightly thickened and bubbly, then cook and stir for 1 minute more.
1 6½-ounce can tuna 3 slices process Swiss *or* American cheese, torn into pieces	● Drain tuna. Using a fork, flake tuna into soup. Add cheese. Cook and stir till cheese is melted and soup is heated through. Set aside desired portions. (See *Dashing Diners*.) Makes 4 servings.

Dashing Diners: Cover and chill set-aside portions of soup. Before serving, place soup in a saucepan. Cook and stir the mixture over medium heat till it is heated through.

Lemony Almond Fish

EQUIPMENT

aluminum foil
small saucepan
knife
shredder
juicer
measuring spoons
dry measures
wooden spoon
liquid measure
baking sheet
hot pads

To toast almonds, place them in a single layer in a shallow baking pan. Bake in a 350° oven about 5 minutes or till light brown. Or, place nuts in a 2-cup measure. Microcook on 100% power (high) for 2 to 3 minutes.

- 1 pound orange roughy or flounder fish fillets (about 4)
- 2 tablespoons margarine or butter
- ½ teaspoon finely shredded lemon peel
- 1 tablespoon lemon juice
- 1 teaspoon dried parsley flakes
- ½ teaspoon onion salt
- 1 cup quick-cooking rice

● Divide fish into 4 equal parts, if necessary. Tear four 12-inch squares of foil; fold up edges slightly. In a small saucepan melt margarine or butter. Stir in lemon peel, lemon juice, parsley, and onion salt. Stir in *uncooked* rice. Divide mixture among 4 foil packets.

- ½ cup water
- ⅓ cup sliced almonds, toasted (optional)

● Pour *2 tablespoons* water over each portion of rice. Place *1* fish fillet on top of rice, turning under thin edges to make an even thickness. Sprinkle with almonds, if you like. Bring foil up and over fish on 2 sides. Fold over. Fold other edges in (see photo, right).

Bring 2 opposite sides of foil up together. Fold pieces together, then fold down to fish, as shown. Fold remaining sides toward center of packet.

Lemon wedges (optional)

● Set aside desired number of portions. (See *Dashing Diners*.) Place packets on a baking sheet. Bake in a 450° oven for 8 to 10 minutes for ½-inch fillets (or about 15 minutes for ¾-inch fillets). Serve with lemon wedges, if you like. Serves 4.

Dashing Diners: Do not bake set-aside portions. Place foil packets in the refrigerator till serving time. Continue as directed.

Home-Run Ham Patties

EQUIPMENT
can opener
12-inch skillet
pancake turner
paper towels
small bowl
dry measures
measuring spoons
spoon
knife
cutting board
aluminum foil

These patties were a big hit with Melvin, one of our tasters. He gave it a top score and said it was his favorite of all the foods he tasted.

1 12-ounce can ham patties (6) *or* 12 ounces thinly sliced fully cooked ham	● Set aside desired number of patties. (See *Dashing Diners*.) In a 12-inch skillet cook remaining patties over medium heat about 4 minutes or till light brown; turn once (if using thinly sliced ham, cook for 1 to 2 minutes). Drain on paper towels, if necessary.
¼ cup plain yogurt 1 tablespoon sweet pickle relish ½ teaspoon prepared mustard	● For dressing, in a small bowl stir together yogurt, pickle relish, and mustard. Set aside desired portion of dressing.
3 large pita bread rounds Leaf lettuce 1 medium cucumber, thinly sliced	● Cut pitas in half and open pockets. Set aside desired number of pita halves. Line each remaining half with lettuce and 2 or 3 cucumber slices. Place 1 ham patty or several slices of ham in each pita half. Dollop each with dressing. Makes 6 servings.

Dashing Diners: Wrap *uncooked* patties in foil. Chill. Cover set-aside dressing. Chill. To serve, prepare as directed above.

Hero for a Day

Stacked with thinly sliced meat, fresh veggies, and choice cheeses, this sandwich will make you a hero with everyone. As maker of the meal, you'll have fun putting this hearty suppertime sandwich together. Top off the meal with Waldorf Slaw and a glass of ice-cold milk. (See recipes, pages 92 and 93.)

MENU

Hearty Hero Sandwich
Waldorf Slaw
Milk

MENU COUNTDOWN

45 Minutes Ahead:
Prepare Waldorf Slaw. Cover and chill.
30 Minutes Ahead:
Prepare dressing for Hearty Hero Sandwich. Assemble sandwich.
5 Minutes Ahead:
Pour milk into mugs.

Hearty Hero Sandwich

Pictured on pages 90 and 91.

EQUIPMENT
small bowl
spoon
dry measures
measuring spoons
bread knife
fork
knife
wooden skewers

Say cheese—and experiment with Colby, Swiss, provolone, Muenster, or Monterey Jack instead of traditional American or cheddar for your next hero.

¼ cup mayonnaise *or* salad dressing
1 tablespoon dry onion soup mix
1 tablespoon milk
1 teaspoon prepared mustard

- In a small bowl stir together mayonnaise or salad dressing, dry onion soup mix, milk, and mustard. Let stand for 15 minutes.

1 16-ounce loaf *unsliced* French bread
Leaf lettuce
1 cup potato salad

- Halve French bread horizontally. Using a fork, lightly scrape and remove bread from loaf bottom. If you like, also remove some of the bread from the loaf top. Line bottom with lettuce. Spoon potato salad onto lettuce.

8 ounces sliced fully cooked ham, turkey, *or* roast beef
2 ounces sliced salami *or* summer sausage
6 ounces sliced cheese
2 small tomatoes, thinly sliced

- Layer meat, salami or summer sausage, cheese, and tomatoes onto potato salad. Spread top with mayonnaise mixture. Place top, spread side down, on sandwich. Place 4 wooden skewers along length of hero. Cut into 4 sections. Makes 4 servings.

Waldorf Slaw

Pictured on page 90.

EQUIPMENT
large bowl	dry measures
knife	measuring spoons
shredder	small bowl
cutting board	spoon

1½ cups coarsely shredded cabbage
1 small apple, cored and cut into bite-size pieces
¼ cup chopped celery
¼ cup shredded carrot
2 tablespoons raisins
2 tablespoons walnuts

● In a large bowl combine cabbage, apple, celery, carrot, raisins, and nuts.

⅓ cup plain yogurt
⅓ cup mayonnaise *or* salad dressing
1 teaspoon sugar
½ teaspoon celery seed

● In a small bowl combine yogurt, mayonnaise or salad dressing, sugar, and celery seed. Pour over cabbage mixture; toss to mix. Cover and chill. Serves 4.

The saying goes, "If you can't beat 'em, join 'em!" So, that's exactly what we did to make one winning taste from two favorite salads. Half coleslaw and half Waldorf Salad, this refreshing side dish has shredded cabbage, apple chunks, plump raisins, and crunchy walnuts.

Index

A-B

All-American Cheeseburgers, 56
Anytime Snowballs, 43
Applesauce, Rosy-Posy, 26
Apricot Muffins, Mighty, 27
Apricot Spread, 27
Baked Ham with Plum Sauce, 58
Banana Bites, Frozen, 48
Beef
    All-American Cheeseburgers, 56
    Beef 'n' Swiss Spread, 49
    Spaghetti and Meatballs, 84
    Whole-in-One Pizza, 78
Beverages
    Berry Bash, 36
    CC Shake, 37
    Chocolate-Banana Fizz, 14
    Cocoa Loco, 15
    Cranberry Catch, 13
    Marvelous Melon Shake, 16
    Peachy Keen Slush, 36
    Peanut-Chocolate Shake, 42
    Pep Rally Pineapple Shake, 13
    Space Shake, 42
    Tangy Fruit Tempters, 37
    Tomato Tune-Up, 13
    Triple Dream Shake, 13
    Yummy Yogurt Gulp, 16
Breads
    Cheese Fingers, 82
    Ham and Cheddar Horns, 21
    Jam and Biscuits, 25
    Mighty Apricot Muffins, 27
    Sugar-and-Spice Twirls, 26
Butter Pecan Pudding, 46
By-the-Sea Chowder, 87
By-the-Slice Pizza, 70

C-E

Candy, Ice Cream and, 41
CC Shake, 37
Cheese
    Beef 'n' Swiss Spread, 49
    Cheese and Carrot Corps, 8
    Cheese Fingers, 82
    Cheese Wheels, 24
    Cheesewiches, 32
    Cheesy Bagelwich, 31
    Cheesy Tater Pie, 53
    Ham 'n' Cheddar Spread, 49
    Never-Better Nachos, 17
    Quesadillas, 19
    Turkey 'n' Mozzarella Spread, 49
Chicken
    Chicken Bundles, 64
    Chicken Curls, 52
    Chicken Tacos, 83
    Dilled Fried Chicken, 62
    Lemon Chicken, 57
    Orange-Chicken Delight, 80
    Orange-Maple Chicken, 54
    Saucy Chicken Cups, 86
Chili Skillet, 50
Chocolate
    Chocolate-Banana Fizz, 14
    Chocolate Chippers, 34
    Cocoa Loco, 15
    Peanut-Chocolate Shake, 42
Cocoa Loco, 15
Confetti Spread, 31
Cookies
    Chocolate Chippers, 34
    Crunchy Peanut Butter Cookies, 47
Country Casserole, 63
Couscous Salad, 62
Cranberries and Turkey, 81
Creamy Ham and Veggies, 79
Crunchy Peanut Butter Cookies, 47
Dandy Candy Whirl, 18
Desserts
    Peanutty Stuffed Pears, 71
    Pudding Pie Squares, 44
Dilled Fried Chicken, 62
Dips and Spreads
    Beef 'n' Swiss Spread, 49
    Confetti Spread, 31
    Ham 'n' Cheddar Spread, 49
    Mucho-Gusto Munchies, 38
    Orange-Pineapple Fruit Dip, 24
    Tangy Fruit Fluff, 18
    Turkey 'n' Mozzarella Spread, 49
Drum Rolls, 8
Dusty Popcorn, 10
Easy Potato-Sausage Chowder, 76
Eggs
    Egg-Salad Roll Ups, 73
    Scrambled Sandwich, 28

F-L

Fife and Drum Dip, 8
Firecrackers, 8
Fish and Seafood
    By-the-Sea Chowder, 87
    Lemony Almond Fish, 88
    Orange-Poached Fish, 77
Frozen Pops
    CC Shake, 37
    Great Grape Fruit Pops, 43
    PB&J Shake and Shiver, 40
    Tangy Fruit Tempters, 37
Fruit
    Frozen Banana Bites, 48
    Fruit-and-Nut Nibble Mix, 7
    Fruit Kabobs, 23

Fruit *(continued)*
    Fruit Stack-Ups, 29
    Orange-Pineapple Fruit Dip, 24
    Peanutty Stuffed Pears, 71
    Rosy-Posy Applesauce, 26
    Tangy Fruit Fluff, 18
    Very Berry Parfaits, 11
Garden Salad, 71
German Spuds, 75
Great Grape Fruit Pops, 43
Ham
    Baked Ham with Plum Sauce, 58
    Cheesy Tater Pie, 53
    Country Casserole, 63
    Creamy Ham and Veggies, 79
    Ham and Cheddar Horns, 21
    Ham 'n' Cheddar Spread, 49
    Home-Run Ham Patties, 89
Hearty Hero Sandwich, 92
Home-Run Ham Patties, 89
Ice Cream
    Anytime Snowballs, 43
    Dandy Candy Whirl, 18
    Ice Cream and Candy, 41
Italian Taters, 75
Lemon Chicken, 57
Lemony Almond Fish, 88

M-O

Main Dishes
    All-American Cheeseburgers, 56
    Baked Ham with Plum Sauce, 58
    By-the-Sea Chowder, 87
    By-the-Slice Pizza, 70
    Cheesy Tater Pie, 53
    Chicken Bundles, 64
    Chicken Curls, 52
    Chicken Tacos, 83
    Chili Skillet, 50

Main Dishes *(continued)*
    Country Casserole, 63
    Cranberries and Turkey, 81
    Creamy Ham and Veggies, 79
    Dilled Fried Chicken, 62
    Easy Potato-Sausage Chowder, 76
    Egg-Salad Roll Ups, 73
    Hearty Hero Sandwich, 92
    Home-Run Ham Patties, 89
    Lemon Chicken, 57
    Lemony Almond Fish, 88
    Orange-Chicken Delight, 80
    Orange-Maple Chicken, 54
    Orange-Poached Fish, 77
    Pork Loaf with Cranberry Sauce, 67
    Saucy Chicken Cups, 86
    Saucy Sausage Skillet, 55
    Sausage Soup, 82
    Scrambled Sandwich, 28
    Spaghetti and Meatballs, 84
    Spanish-Style Pork Chops, 58
    Super Spuds, 74
    Tempting Tuna Salad, 72
    Tuna Turnovers, 59
    Turkey and Trimmings, 66
    Whole-in-One Pizza, 78
Make-Ahead Snacks
    Anytime Snowballs, 43
    Butter Pecan Pudding, 46
    Crunchy Peanut Butter Cookies, 47
    Frozen Banana Bites, 48
    Great Grape Fruit Pops, 43
    Ham 'n' Cheddar Spread, 49
    Peanut-Chocolate Shake, 42
    Pudding Pie Squares, 44
    Space Shake, 42

Marvelous Melon Shake, 16
Menus
    Favorite Fried Chicken, 60
    Hero for a Day, 90
    Mamma Mia, It's a Pizza!, 69
Mighty Apricot Muffins, 27
Mucho-Gusto Munchies, 38
Muffins, Mighty Apricot, 27
Nachos, Never-Better, 17
Orange-Chicken Delight, 80
Orange-Maple Chicken, 54
Orange-Pineapple Fruit Dip, 24
Orange-Poached Fish, 77

P-R

PB&J Shake and Shiver, 40
Peachy Keen Slush, 36
Peanut Butter
    Cheese and Carrot Corps, 8
    Drum Rolls, 8
    Fife and Drum Dip, 8
    Firecrackers, 8
    Peanut-Chocolate Shake, 42
    Spirited Spread, 8
Peanutty Stuffed Pears, 71
Pie à la Mode Waffles, 30
Pizza, By-the-Slice, 70
Pizza, Whole-in-One, 78
Popcorn
    Dusty Popcorn, 10
    Tropical Teasers, 40
Pork Chops, Spanish-Style, 58
Pork Loaf with Cranberry Sauce, 67
Potatoes
    Easy Potato-Sausage Chowder, 76
    German Spuds, 75
    Italian Taters, 75
    Potatoes O'Connor, 75
    Super Spuds, 74
    Texas Taters, 75

Pudding
  Butter Pecan Pudding, 46
  Pudding Pie Squares, 44
  Tropical Teasers, 40
Pumpkin-Pie Party Mix, 33
Quesadillas, 19
Quick Takes
  Chocolate-Banana Fizz, 14
  Cocoa Loco, 15
  Dandy Candy Whirl, 18
  Dusty Popcorn, 10
  Fruit-and-Nut Nibble Mix, 7
  Marvelous Melon Shake, 16
  Never-Better Nachos, 17
  Quesadillas, 19
  Tangy Fruit Fluff, 18
  Tic-Tac-Taco Mix, 7
  Tomato Tune-Up, 13
  Triple Dream Shake, 13
  Veggie Pickpockets, 11
  Very Berry Parfaits, 11
  Yummy Yogurt Gulp, 16
Rosy-Posy Applesauce, 26

S-Z

Salads
  Couscous Salad, 62
  Garden Salad, 71
  Tempting Tuna Salad, 72
  Waldorf Slaw, 93
Sandwiches
  Cheesewiches, 32
  Hearty Hero Sandwich, 92
  Home-Run Ham Patties, 89
  Salad on a Bun, 22
  Scrambled Sandwich, 28
Saucy Chicken Cups, 86

Saucy Sausage Skillet, 55
Sausage
  Easy Potato-Sausage Chowder, 76
  Saucy Sausage Skillet, 55
  Sausage Soup, 82
  Sweet 'n' Sour Bites, 29
Scrambled Sandwich, 28
Shakes
  CC Shake, 37
  Chocolate-Banana Fizz, 14
  Cranberry Catch, 13
  Dandy Candy Whirl, 18
  Marvelous Melon Shake, 16
  PB&J Shake and Shiver, 40
  Peanut-Chocolate Shake, 42
  Pep Rally Pineapple Shake, 13
  Space Shake, 42
  Triple Dream Shake, 13
  Yummy Yogurt Gulp, 16
Snack Mixes
  Fruit-and-Nut Nibble Mix, 7
  Pumpkin-Pie Party Mix, 33
  Tic-Tac-Taco Mix, 7
Soups
  By-the-Sea Chowder, 87
  Easy Potato-Sausage Chowder, 76
  Sausage Soup, 82
Space Shake, 42
Spaghetti and Meatballs, 84
Spanish-Style Pork Chops, 58
Spirited Spread, 8
Sugar-and-Spice Twirls, 26
Sugar-and-Spice Waffles, 30
Super Spuds, 74
Sweet 'n' Sour Bites, 29
Tacos, Chicken, 83
Tangy Fruit Fluff, 18
Tangy Fruit Tempters, 37
Tempting Tuna Salad, 72
Texas Taters, 75
Tic-Tac-Taco Mix, 7

Tomato Tune-Up, 13
Triple Dream Shake, 13
Tropical Teasers, 40
Tuna
  By-the-Sea Chowder, 87
  Tempting Tuna Salad, 72
  Tuna Turnovers, 59
Turkey
  Cranberries and Turkey, 81
  Turkey and Trimmings, 66
  Turkey 'n' Mozzarella Spread, 49
Veggie Pickpockets, 11
Very Berry Parfaits, 11
Waffles
  Pie à la Mode Waffles, 30
  Sugar-and-Spice Waffles, 30
  Wonderful Wafflewich, 30
  Yo-Go Waffles, 30
Waldorf Slaw, 93
Whole-in-One Pizza, 78
Wonderful Wafflewich, 30
Yo-Go Waffles, 30
Yummy Yogurt Gulp, 16

Tips

Make It Micro!, 32
Shake It!, 14
The Tops in "Pops," 10